THE
Dressage Rider's Survival Guide

Memoirs of a Struggling
Dressage Rider

THE
Dressage Rider's Survival Guide

Memoirs of a Struggling Dressage Rider

By Margaret A. Odgers

Illustrations by Eva Sandor

Half Halt Press, Inc.
Boonsboro, Maryland

The Dressage Rider's Survival Guide:
Memoirs of a Struggling Dressage Rider
©2004 Margaret A. Odgers

Published in the United States of America by
Half Halt Press, Inc.
P.O. Box 67
Boonsboro, MD 21713
www.halfhaltpress.com

Cover and interior design by Design Point, Epping, NH
Cover and interior illustrations by Eva Sandor
Editorial services by Stacey Nedrow-Wigmore

Printed in The United States of America

Library of Congress Cataloging-in-Publication Data

Odgers, Margaret A., 1970-
        The dressage rider's survival guide: memoirs of a
        struggling dressage rider / by Margaret A. Odgers ;
        illustrations by Eva Sandor.
            p. cm.
        Includes bibliographical references (p.).
        ISBN 0-939481-70-7 (Pbk)
        1. Odgers, Margaret A., 1970- 2. Dressage riders--
        Pennsylvania--Biography. 3. Dressage--Pennsylvania--
        Anecdotes. 4. Dressage--Pennsylvania--Humor. I. Title.

SF309.482.O44A3 2004
798.2'3'092—dc22
[B]
                                                    2004054070

DEDICATION

Dedicated to the
Nokota Horse Conservancy, Inc.
www.nokotahorse.org

This book is dedicated to the Nokota Horse Conservancy, Inc. As a writer, I'm embarrassed to admit that I can't find the words to adequately express my deep appreciation for the Nokota horses and my admiration for the people who struggle so hard to preserve them. But I must mention brothers Leo Kuntz and Frank Kuntz, the founders of the conservancy.

For nearly 25 years, these men have taken on the task of preserving and protecting the Nokotas—the last wild horses of North Dakota who now reside on the Kuntz family ranch in Linton, North Dakota. These unique horses are the descendents of the Indian ponies of Chief Sitting Bull and the Indian-cross horses used by the early settlers of the Northern Plains. The painstaking efforts of the Kuntz family to save this breed have won the admiration of many, including my family. If only the world had more people like you.

I am donating a portion of the proceeds from this book to the Nokota Horse Conservancy. So even if you hate the book, at least you can know you've helped a very deserving cause! ❑

TABLE OF CONTENTS

ACKNOWLEDGEMENTS

I must thank the many people who supported my efforts in bringing *Survival Guide* to life. First of all, thanks to Elizabeth Carnes, publisher of Half Halt Press, Inc., for taking a chance on a first-time writer.

Thanks to Mark Susol and the members of Ultimate Dressage Bulletin Board (UDBB) for so enthusiastically supporting *Survival Guide*. In particular, thanks to UDBB members Lynne Flaherty, for her humorous foreword, and Eva Sandor, for her wonderful and funny illustrations.

Thanks are also in order to the members of UDBB who gave their permission to be quoted in *Survival Guide*. Their real-world description of the thrills and the pitfalls of dressage give invaluable, and sometimes hysterically funny, perspective into the practice of this art form. Here they are along with their UDBB board names: V. Boyd (Apples), E. Buck (spirithorse), C. Budd (twotempi01), M. Dickinson (ToN Farm), S. Givens (class), L. Graham (JumperCash), K. Hall (galliegirl), Kathy Johnson, D. Kammer (Trakehner Addict), Paula Kierkegaard (galopp), V. Luther (Vee), S. Marshall (Little Jamie), C. Monto (goneriding), T. Prevo (EquusTP), P. Rothschild (Peter Guy), B. Sanford (AndalusianMom), Monica Sellers (Monica S), J. Simpson (Zoeneens), L. Smithson (SmithsonLM), Lynne Sprinsky (Lynne S), G. Stubbs (sunrider), G. Walker (horseaddict), Katherine Wildey (Katherine), M. Yates (Dressagerose).

Thanks, of course, to my family. They put up with a lot of hastily thrown together dinners while I was immersed in writing this book. To my very dear, ever supportive, nonhorsey husband, Chris—I love you, sweetheart! Thanks to my daughter Kat, one of the best little horsewomen I know. And to my twin sons, Alex and Nick—you two light up the room, and my heart, with your presence.

And finally, thanks so much to my dearest friend in the whole world, Pam Pew. You held my hand through this from beginning to end. You supported and inspired so much of this book. Friends like you are one of life's greatest treasures. ❏

Margaret Odgers
(Mao2)

IN APOLOGY

As a guilt-ridden dressage rider, I'd also like to take this opportunity to apologize to all my horses past and present:

Shamrock and B.G.: The horses of my childhood.
In the Stone Age, before dressage, I cherish the memories!

Bolero and Creedence: The horses of my
Hack Stable Queen years.
When trail riding ruled! Ah, what fun we had!

Sassy: Although not mine, you were my
informal introduction to dressage.
(I'm really, *really* sorry!)

Chad and Gus: My first and second
(but not last) dressage horses.
You both suffered a lot but were great sports! To Chad, in particular, I'm sorry about the draw reins. Thankfully, you are both in homes where you won't face a "Black Beauty" future. Thank you, Susan and Liana.

Chico: My daughter's Nokota horse.
Your impact on our family has been amazing and I admire you above all others. You are a steadfast friend and formidable enemy (ha!), bold and affectionate, funny and wise, and, all in all, quite a remarkable character.

And, I hear you. Quit with the 20-meter circles and let the girlie-girl ride!

Poster Boy, Teddy and Moonshine: My Nokota foster horses. For your incredible patience with my version of dressage training while I seek out your new wonderful homes. You all have taught me more than I could ever possibly hope to teach you.

And finally, to my Andalusian **Capricho**, who deserves the biggest apology of all.
It goes without saying that you deserve better, but no one will appreciate your mane and tail like I do! You are
The Fabulous One—forever immortalized as TFO.

***

To each and every one of you, I'm so sorry for all the times I've pulled back on the reins. Horses *are* the most magnificent and generous creatures on earth. ❏

FOREWORD
A GUIDE TO APPORTIONING BLAME
By Lynne Flaherty, M.D.

Yes, you have bought another dressage book. This tells us something about you. You are a dressage book buyer, which means you are still in search of the Holy Grail. Most likely, you will read the first two chapters of this book and decide that it, too, is unlikely to lead you to nirvana (or the perfect piaffe or getting the left lead canter). Unlike those other books that make you feel so guilty, *Survival Guide* strives to be a useful book. Therefore, we have decided to begin it with the ending, which is how you justify spending so much time and money on something and never get any better at it. Accordingly, here is your guide to:

APPORTIONING BLAME

It is a sad but incontrovertible fact that the vast majority of dressage riders will puddle around at Training Level and maybe First

Level for their entire riding lives. It doesn't matter who you are, how much money you have or who teaches you. An article in *Practical Horseman* many years ago talked about Kathleen Raine's mother, Betsy, who "with an eye educated by twenty-eight years of lessons with [Olympian] Hilda Gurney, shows in lower-level dressage." And, if Kathleen Raine's mother, with access to horses in Europe, a teacher like Hilda Gurney and a well known daughter who rides at the highest levels in the sport can't get out of the lower levels, neither, most likely, will you.

This causes a problem because you are undoubtedly much like the rest of us dressage riders: you have invested a good portion of your self-worth in this frustrating activity. Failure to progress can cause depression, demoralization and a profound feeling of worthlessness, which is not even ameliorated by chocolate. Therefore, every dressage rider must spend the time necessary to construct the proper defense against these feelings. This consists of accurately apportioning the blame for one's failure.

The Trainer

This is an easy one. Most everybody has a trainer, and if you don't have a trainer, then the lack of one is the immediate—and pretty valid—explanation for your failure to progress. If you do have a trainer, however, it's necessary to explain why the trainer has failed to get you where you want to go.

It may be that your trainer has a stable full of stalled-out amateurs. This gives you a clear explanation: Your trainer is good with beginners, but he or she doesn't have the experience, background or teaching ability to bring someone along. Perhaps your trainer has never ridden much beyond where you are now. (In which case, *what* are you doing giving her your money, may we ask?) The problem with this excuse is that it's only good for a short time, after which people will want to know why you haven't changed trainers.

If you are riding with a trainer who *has* had some success bringing students up the levels, you have to be more creative. Perhaps the trainer doesn't like you or doesn't spend any time on you. Perhaps the trainer doesn't like your horse (sometimes this is actually true). If you have an unusual breed of horse, you can always use the idea that the trainer is not good with Lipizzaners, or whatever you have. "Oh, yes, Jeremy does well with the warmbloods, but you know it takes a *special* kind of trainer to work with the Baroque horses." Delivered with the proper disdain, this will buy you quite a bit of time, particularly if there is no trainer working with Lipizzaners in your area.

Another approach is to decide at approximately one to two-year intervals that your current trainer is abusive and your horse is all messed up. You change barns and loudly sing the praises of the new trainer, while explaining to all within earshot that your horse's progress has stopped because "we have to go back to the basics and redo all that work." What makes this strategy amusing to the onlooker is that, at the same time, several people have relocated from your new trainer to your old trainer and are loudly proclaiming the same thing.

A nearly bombproof excuse is to decide that *no* local trainer meets your needs and that you will exclusively clinic with Herr von

Pferdemist. Since Herr von Pferdemist only comes to your area for two or three days a year, this limits the instruction you can get and will obviously impede your progress. And you can look down your nose at the people around you who are riding with local trainers and (gasp!) showing at Second Level because they are not *classical* and therefore not *correct*. You may take the next five years to get out of the walk, but by golly, you are doing it *right*.

The Facility

Boarding is problematic for most of us. Owning horses without property seems to be a constant low-level migration in search of a place with the right combination of horse care, teaching, arenas and footing, and fellow boarders. Along the way, various impediments to dressage progress can be encountered.

If you board in a mixed-discipline barn, you can blame your lack of progress on those annoying hunter people who have *jumps* up in the arena all week. "How can we work on our half passes when the arena is full of poles and standards?" (Never mind that you can't work on your half passes in an empty arena because you don't know how to do them. Said in the proper tone, this will convince.) Or you can explain how your delicate warmblood's sensitive temperament has been traumatized from avoiding sliding stops. I broke young horses at one point in a facility with a reining trainer who worked with Paints. Do you have any idea what the reaction of a pampered, 3-year-old Oldenburg is to an odd-colored horse that is spinning wildly around?

You may board in a facility with poor footing and use that as an explanation for why you have never developed a medium trot. "I'd be running the risk of a suspensory injury for sure!" Perhaps your facility has no mirrors: "I just can't correct my position because I can't see what I'm doing." Perhaps the only boarding stable with adequate facilities is far away: "We'd be doing better except, with the hour-and-a-half drive to the barn, I can only get there three days a week."

In general, facility blaming isn't a strong strategy. There is too much danger that either one of your fellow boarders *will* make progress and show you up, or someone will want to know why you haven't moved if the place you are in is causing you so much trouble.

The Horse

This is a gold mine. The number of shortcomings that can be attributed to the horse is virtually without number. After all, it is the horse's job to do this dressage stuff, isn't it? If he isn't doing it, it's got to be his fault.

Probably the most commonly used excuse is that you have the wrong horse altogether. "You know, I started in the hunters, and that's what Dobbin was good at. He just isn't suited for this dressage stuff." Dobbin may be built downhill, is the wrong breed or has the wrong gaits. Having a gaited horse is foolproof for this! Many riders use the excuse that their horses are not warmbloods. There are two problems with this: Knowledgeable people will give you many examples of horses of the same breed that have been successful in dressage. Your colleagues will eventually tire of hearing your complaints and challenge you to acquire a warmblood, which will nullify your excuse altogether.

The horse's conformation can give you some excuses. "He doesn't step under well, so it's going to take a long time to teach him to collect." When a long time becomes 20 years, it starts to look like something else was also missing. "He has a long, slender neck, so we have to be careful about overflexing him." This will only excuse the fact that he is completely inverted to a fairly naïve audience.

"He doesn't *like* dressage." This is a good excuse for the rider who has decided to abandon the entire undertaking. No one will think less of you for deciding to keep your beloved horse and give up your preferred discipline. The fact that most horses don't care at all what kind of work they do and would simply prefer to do less of it, is rarely mentioned in these circumstances.

"He has a difficult temperament." Most of the time, this translates into, "He really objects to whatever training technique we are currently employing." Into this category fall the youngster who won't go forward (while the rider is gripping with her knees for dear life or balancing on the reins) and the explosive off-the-track Thoroughbred (whose owner is gripping with her knees for dear life and balancing on the reins).

Approaching horse-related excuses from a slightly different angle, you can buy tremendous amounts of time with injuries. Now, dressage horses *do* get injuries—real ones that can result in long layoffs and tedious rehabilitation. Would-be critics will back off promptly when they see you laboriously trudging through the arena footing, doing the prescribed hand-walking after yet another tendon or ligament strain.

However, if your horse has not been cooperative enough to sustain an injury that is convincing, you can take the other approach. You can insist that *something* is wrong with your horse. You can feel it. The horse has odd symptoms like constantly rubbing his face on his right front leg after canter departs. You are certain the horse is in pain. It is a sign of how insensitive your trainer is that he maintains this is a training issue. You can spend much time and even more money in search of the miracle vet who will actually diagnose the problem. The veterinary literature calls this "hypochondria by proxy" and reaps enormous profits from it. Again your critics will be silenced because no one can really fault an owner for diligently working to keep her horse comfortable. Of course, when it's the fourth horse you have had with an ill-defined health problem, they'll be whispering behind your back.

The big advantage of all the horse-related excuses is that you get enormous brownie points from your audience for loving the horse enough to accept his shortcomings (even if they are actually yours) and being content to muddle about with the hoi polloi, rather than selling him to a Black Beauty future so that you can wear a top hat and tails.

Circumstances

So then, what do you do if your horse is talented, your trainer is gifted and you are boarding at a lovely place entirely conducive to dressage? How do you keep the responsibility for your failure to progress from landing in your lap?

Well, there are always the "unfortunate circumstances." Perhaps your husband has been laid off, and there is no money for lessons. Perhaps your employer is asking for lots of overtime and there is no time to ride. Maybe the weather has been so bad that the arena is an ice skating rink. If you are running out of circumstantial excuses, you can always get pregnant (at least the young can do this).

Money-related excuses are great because almost nobody has an unlimited supply of income. Should you be fortunate enough to have the resources for good instruction and training, you can deal with that easily enough by acquiring more horses. It is axiomatic that there will, eventually, come a number of horses that squeeze your budget. It is also nearly axiomatic that most dressage addicts with large pocketbooks will at some point collect that many horses. Since horses are far easier to purchase than to resell, this budget limitation problem may last many years.

Family is another good one. After the birth of the first child, there are so many demands on a mother's time that riding can legitimately be put on a back burner. This is a good, long-term excuse, since it is valid until the youngest child is a teenager. And given some teenagers, it may be valid far longer than that. It is, however, difficult to convince someone that you can't make your riding lesson because you are babysitting your grandchildren, so this excuse eventually has to end.

But about the time that family no longer suffices, you can invoke the best excuse of all: age. Characterizing yourself as middle-aged and arthritic in a self-deprecating tone elicits sympathy and humor from your audience. All vestiges of harsh judgment and criticism fall away as the listener shudders with horror and imagines the day when she, too, will be too stiff to sit the trot. Rarely, if ever, does anyone remember that six-time German Olympian, Dr. Reiner Klimke competed into his 60s, or that the oldest Olympic dressage rider was 76. Age has the additional value of becoming more, rather than less, convincing an excuse as time goes on. Unfortunately, age also has the downside of being a real reason for deteriorating riding, and one you can't fix by finding a new trainer, buying a new horse or moving to another barn.

What it all boils down to is that you need to be quick on your feet and creative to deflect the responsibility for your own shortcomings. This is true in all fields of life. What is unique about dressage is that every day, you will be faced with your failings as a rider every time you swing a leg over your horse. With luck, employing some of the strategies discussed above will help repair your shattered self-esteem.

Or you could take up golf.

Best wishes on your journey. ❏

Lynne Flaherty

"When God created the horse he said to the magnificent creature: I have made thee as no other. All the treasures of the earth lie between thy eyes. Thou shalt carry my friends upon thy back. Thy saddle shall be the seat of prayers to me. And thou fly without wings, and conquer without any sword. Oh, horse."

The Holy Qu'ran (Koran)

PROLOGUE:
A Conversation at IHOP

"I'm going to be sick! Who do I think I am, anyway? I'm not good enough for this horse! He's so beautiful and talented—I know I'll ruin him! He deserves better than me! I should just forget this whole idea of buying an Andalusian! God!" Pam wails. With that, she leaps up from the table and rushes to the restroom. Apparently she really is going to get sick.

Hmm, sounds like some serious self esteem issues. I am sitting at the International House of Pancakes (IHOP) restaurant, waiting patiently for my old and dear friend to return the table. I'm totally unfazed by her seemingly remarkable lack of confidence. We are on a horse-hunting trip, and Pam is merely looking to buy a new dressage horse. This would explain her otherwise puzzling behavior.

Pam and I have been riding buddies since our early 20s. Back then we both labored under the naïve assumption we knew how to ride. Ha, youth! Pam literally grew up riding, though without much formal instruction. She grew up on a small farm in Chester County, Pennsylvania, and began riding when she was 7 years old. Her parents, although certainly not wealthy, were creative in allowing their two girls to enjoy the privileges of riding. Each fall, they'd bring home several horses from the local riding cam,p free of charge, to ride during the off season.

Pam and her sister rode from autumn to spring, hacking about the countryside, wading in creeks, jumping over logs and often riding bareback. For a horse-crazy kid, it was heaven. In her bedroom, Pam hung pictures of beautiful Andalusian horses, a far cry from the sturdy and serviceable camp horses that were her childhood companions. One picture in particular, of a gorgeous white stallion, hung on the ceiling above her bed—the first thing she saw when she woke up—an Andalusian stallion. Her dream horse.

I grew up in the same area, the youngest of four, and the only girl, in a typical middle class suburban neighborhood—the four bedroom, two-and-a-half-bath Colonial on an acre. Much to my parents' bemusement, their only daughter was obsessive over all things to do with horses. No one else in my immediate or extended family had exhibited this particular eccentricity. Of course, my grandfather did like to bet on the ponies and spent a lot of time hanging around the racetrack, but that hardly qualifies, I believe.

Horse books and model horses were a sure winner at birthdays and Christmas. My parents finally gave in to my incessant pleading when I was 9 years old and enrolled me in riding lessons. A dream come true! And as my obsession continued unabated, they actually bought me a horse of my very own when I was 13 years old. It was my Christmas present, a complete surprise, and a memory I will always cherish.

Pam and I also shared a common bond forged by the timeless childhood classic story, *The Black Stallion*, by Walter Farley. *The Black Stallion* is defining literature for horse-crazy kids. It embraces all the romanticism and beauty possible in horses. The young protagonist, Alec Ramsey, overcomes insurmountable odds. It is a parallel perhaps for the impossibility of most of us ever owning a horse of our own, let alone a stunningly beautiful, blazingly fast, jet black, wild Arabian stallion. Even better, Alec was the only one who could ride The Black. The impact of the story of Alec and The Black on *little girls* is somewhat puzzling though, seeing as how our hero, well, is a boy.

As is the way of these things, both Pam and I, like many of our ilk, eventually lost our obsession with horses. Yes, indeed, hormones and puberty finally defeated the horse, and boys became the new fixation. I know my parents breathed a collective sigh of relief, for although they supported me in my horse mania, they never really understood it: Big, dangerous, dirty, expensive beasts—whatever could be the attraction? The obsession with boys—likewise unexplainable beasts at times—was far more understandable (and I say this only and fondly as the mother of young sons—admiring and somewhat envious of their bravado and spirit).

Horses, though, are an insidious disease. Just when my parents saw me safely through my college years and I launched myself into the new world of young adulthood, the ugly obsession reared its head again. I began riding at the local hack stable, which had the benefit of being near a huge national park and offered English saddles. It was there I met Pam, also a young 20-something just finishing college.

Pam and I, although lacking the polish of the local show riders, could really stick on those rough and ready hack horses. We quickly rose to the top of the hack stable heap and graduated to becoming trail guides which is truly the pinnacle of our riding careers to date. (And I mean that.) Our arrogance at this achievement would rival that of any Dressage Queen, despite our faded jeans and dirty sneakers. How we looked down our nose at all those hapless riders bouncing about the hack horses backs.

I rode Midnight, an aged jet black Quarter Horse mare with two speeds—walk and gallop. She was the fastest horse at the stable, which was her finest quality. Only the best could stay on Midnight and it was an honor and a thrill to ride her. Pam rode April, a beautiful gray Quarter Horse mare, noted for her "turbo" thrust and a tendency to buck. April was the only horse that could give Midnight a run for her money. April, like Midnight, was strictly a "guide" horse. Now this was riding! This was fun!

Alas, those glory days of drag racing our horses through the park would eventually come to an end. Again, "boys" would spell the end to our riding days. This time, instead of double dates and proms, it was marriage and children. Happily, the friendship Pam and I forged through countless hours on horseback endured this new plateau into adulthood. In fact, we have spent countless hours on the phone, jabbering on about horses while our toddlers were crying, whining and demanding attention in the background. Yes, the magic of horses often gave us succor from the rigors of young motherhood.

As our children got older and our hips began their inevitable spread, the allure of riding beckoned once again. But we are older now, responsible for the welfare of our young children. The thrills and spills of hack stable riding were not as appealing and Midnight and April were no longer our mounts of choice. Honed by the discipline of raising kids, we are ripe to try our hand at something new: Dressage.

Pam and I did not realize how very ill-prepared we were for undertaking dressage. After all, we assumed we could ride. Anyone who could stay on Midnight and April could ride. But one of the earliest lessons we learned in dressage is that very, very, *very* few people can ride correctly, and neither of us qualified. We have both seen our self-esteem plummet into the Perma-Flex footing of that rectangular dressage arena. No longer were we the Hack Stable Queens. We were fledging, barely competent dressage novices. And this after a lifetime of riding experience.

So we have floundered our way through the labyrinth of dressage, mostly despairing and occasionally exultant of our progress. At first we thought it was our less-than-correct hack stable/trail riding background that was hampering our progress. Then it was perhaps lack of sufficient time and money. Then it was the inability to find just the right instructor. And then it was obvious that we didn't have suitable horses. Gradually, however, the truth has begun to dawn. All of these reasons were correct. And many of our peers, regardless of their background, are mired in the same dilemma. It is not just us; this is Dressage.

So now, several years and a few horses later, here we are, Pam and I, having breakfast at the ubiquitous IHOP. We are on a fabulous adventure, six hours from home, away from husbands, kids and jobs, on a horse hunting trip. Pam is looking at a lovely Andalusian gelding, her dressage prospect, her dream horse. At this point, we are confirmed adult amateur dressage riders. And this, of course, explains Pam's extraordinary lack of self-esteem.

As we carefully order our breakfast—she's on Atkins, I'm on a low-fat diet—Pam utters her statement, literally sick with fear at buying this horse—the culmination of her lifelong dream. This is the same person who kept a picture of an Andalusian stallion on her girlhood bedroom ceiling. As we hashed out the pros and cons of Pam buying this horse, I came to an epiphany of sorts. Pam's self-doubt regarding her worthiness for this horse mirrored many of my own insecurities. And I realized that, yes, even though I am merely a Training Level dressage rider, I do have something to contribute to learning the art of dressage—how to survive the journey.

This is a cautionary tale. Nearly half a decade into the "dressage journey," three horses and four instructors later, I'm still mired in the lower levels. I considered calling this book, *Dressage: Intro to Training Level—the First Five (?) Years*. How sad is that? So clearly you will not find the answer here on to how to become a successful dressage rider. Far from it. While I still may not have figured out the shoulder-in I have observed that many of my contemporaries, like Pam, have suffered the same difficulties, the same guilt and the same horrible self-doubt I have. Many, I believe, think they are the only ones. I'm here to tell you, you are not alone! It's hard to imagine that this is even a story about horseback riding, given this somber tone. But trust me: If you have attempted dressage, you know exactly what I'm referring to.

I have had my heart broken and been overcome with guilt with each of my dressage horses. There was Chad, the failed resale project, a wonderful little gray Arabian gelding. Chad was the first Arabian I'd ever owned, and I now understand why Arabian owners, in general, are so passionate about this breed. What heart and try these horses have! I don't own Chad anymore.

After Chad, there was Gus, my second dressage horse. Gus was the opposite of Chad in almost every respect (in my attempt to learn from my mistakes, no doubt). Gus was a big, dark bay Thoroughbred/Percheron-cross gelding with the soul of a gentleman and a big, bouncy trot. I don't own Gus anymore.

The next important horse in my dressage saga is Chico, a small gray Nokota gelding. The Nokotas are a rare breed of Indian-cross horses native to North Dakota. These hardy survivors of the formidable Little Missouri Badlands are prized for their versatility, smarts and steel-like durability. I can personally attest that their I.Q. alone is enough to humble the keenest human mind. There have been countless times I wished Chico could talk, so he could give me advice on burning issues of the day. On the other hand, maybe I'd rather not hear his comments regarding dressage and my riding ability.

Fortunately for Chico, he is my daughter Kat's horse and thus safe from getting the ax for lack of dressage suitability. It is through the adventures of Kat and Chico that I've really been able to put my dressage journey in to perspective. They have given me more insight into horses and horsemanship than all the instructors, books and videos combined.

And finally, there is my third, and current (at the time of publishing, that is) dressage horse, Capricho: a small, yet fiery Andalusian gelding. Capricho is referred to as The Fabulous One (TFO for short) and is a legend in his own mind. The vanity of this horse is awe-inspiring. I have often pondered whether to put a full-length mirror opposite his stall so that he can better admire his luxurious forelock, mane and tail along with his overall exquisite beauty.

In TFO, I attempted to distill the best qualities of Chad, Gus and Chico into one horse, with mixed results. But if anyone should question my credentials to write this book, I offer you this: With TFO I have scored multiple times in the 70s at Intro Level, including a 76.5 percent. That's right, I'm right up there with Isabell Werth, Anky van Grunsven and Ulla Salzgeber (No quibbling over test level here! Grand Prix—Intro—it's all about the basics, anyway!)

Despite this glorious achievement, I can assure you that I *still* have no clue what I'm doing. However, my overweening pride at this accomplishment assures its mention in any conversation I have about dressage. Well, to be honest, the conversation doesn't even have to be about dressage. There was the time I ran after the mailman to share my news. He now speeds past my house and throws our mail on the driveway. Perhaps I should have remembered his check at Christmastime? I was hoping to devote a full chapter to my 76.5 score, but editors can be so picky! Therefore, we worked out a compromise. Please turn to the Appendix, where you can see the test for yourself. The original 76.5, after being carefully put under glass, is hanging on my dressage wall of fame/shame at home. I recently added some discreet lighting to beam upon it at all times. Too much?

Having been duly informed of my crowning glory, let us turn back to TFO. Obviously TFO is the one who deserves the bulk of the credit and is a horse of some talent. One would assume that I am, at last, confident that I have the best possible mount to go forward on my dressage journey. Not at all! I can, but won't, recount every excruciating detail of my ongoing frustrations with the training of TFO. I've heard it said (though I wouldn't have a clue) that the most difficult level to break through is from Second to Third Level. Liars! Truly, the most difficult hurdle in dressage is from Intro to Training Level. Forget collection—it's all about the canter! This should give you some inkling then, into the travails of learning dressage.

So, *Survival Guide* seeks to entertain, to commiserate and perhaps even offer a glimmer of understanding. While many more enlightened tomes may offer the key to unlock the secrets of the shoulder-in, with this, I humbly offer merely a shoulder to cry on and someone to share a good laugh over our painfully sincere efforts in the art of surviving dressage. ❑

CHAPTER ONE
Getting Started

So, You Want to Learn Dressage?

> *"The object of dressage is the harmonious development of the physique and ability of the horse. As a result it makes the horse calm, supple, loose and flexible but also confident, attentive and keen thus achieving perfect understanding with his rider."*
> **Rule XIX Dressage Division; Article 1901. Objectives and General Principles,** *U.S. Equestrian Federation Rule Book*

It begins innocently enough: You decide you want to learn to ride dressage, one of the fastest growing equestrian sports in the United States. Images flow through your mind of those fabulous dressage horses, their necks proudly arched, dancing sideways across the sand arena. Soon this will be you! Let us start with one very clear statement: Rest assured, this will *not* be you.

Dressage seems an admirable goal, noble even. Clearly, dressage is one of the most enlightened forms of riding. According to the literature its practice can improve even the lowliest equine partners. Dressage training develops the correct muscling in horses, which enables them to live longer, healthier and happier lives. And those people who undertake the journey are typically the best, most progressive and tactful of riders.

Historical Roots of Dressage in the United States

"There has recently been in North America an explosion of interest in dressage. Although prior American experience with horsemanship has been long, deep and rooted in fundamental love of the horse, it has been primarily a utilitarian relationship ... we have not had a long tradition of riding as an art."
Walter Zettl, *Dressage in Harmony*

Very few dressage riders come from a pure dressage background. Most riders in the United States have done hunter/jumper, Western riding, saddleseat or some mix therein. For centuries, dressage was the domain of the secret horse societies like the Spanish Riding School of Vienna and European cavalry riders, and was very rare in the United States until after World War II. It was then, unbeknownst to the gullible riding public, that a few very accomplished riders from Europe were absorbed into upper-class families in the States.

The mission given to these expatriates was to teach the daughters of the elite the finer points of riding and perhaps school a foxhunter or two. Many of these military riders had the misfortune of being on the losing end of a terrible war. They had poor employment prospects in both their native countries and abroad. Military guys with European accents weren't looked upon favorably during that era, and Americans can't tell one European accent from another. Thanks to the elite, their legacy was protected and today the masses are reaping the benefits of their knowledge. The introduction of dressage in the United States was not, as the more paranoid have implied, a Nazi plot to make ordinary people worship the "Fatherland."

Suddenly, trainers of the superb caliber and unpronounceable names exploded onto the scene. One was the late Bertalan de Nemethy, who coached the U.S. Equestrian Team to rousing success in show jumping. Of course, what he really did was teach them dressage. Mr. de Nemethy, you see, understood how to perform a proper half halt. Learning the half halt had an extraordinary impact on the American show jumping team. No longer were they crashing willy-nilly over, under and through the fences. For the first time in history, American riders were actually clearing the fences with some style, thanks to Mr. de Nemethy, dressage and the half halt.

Unlike Ronald Reagan's experiment with the American economy in the 1980s, this is a case where the classic trickle-down theory has actually worked. Dressage has quietly and insidiously invaded the lower levels of equestrian consciousness, and now, in the 21st Century, it is enjoying immense popularity and recognition. Now everyone wants to learn dressage and the half halt. Learning dressage and the half halt is no longer the exclusive domain of the upper class, except perhaps the FEI International Levels where a few cases of

Snooty European Rider

correct dressage and proper half halts have been documented. At any rate, the bulk of dressage riders riding the lower levels are comprised of surprisingly ordinary, well intentioned, middle-class folks, struggling to grasp the finer points of dressage and the half halt, and of course, emulate our betters.

The Nature and Organization of Dressage

" In the early days of dressage in the United States, the outlook was not very promising. Only one book was available on the subject in the English language. Other translated books which followed confused many riders, instructors and judges. Our first selected dressage riders (officers as well as civilians) had a disadvantage in competition against riders from other countries. "

Fritz Stecken, *Training the Horse and Rider*

The Introduction of the All-Important Intro and Training Levels

Dressage has the appealing feature of measured steps from beginner through advanced levels. The official first level is called, not surprisingly, First Level. The unofficial first level is called Training Level. Training Level was added early in the genesis of dressage in the United States because, clearly, no one here was capable of performing First Level. In order to attract an audience, Training Level was created for riders switching from other disciplines who had an interest in pretending to do dressage. At Training Level, the rider performs at the walk, trot and canter, but there are no dressage requirements. Initially, it was thought that as dressage became more popular, Training Level would be dropped from the repertoire. Quite the opposite has occurred. This has been one case where American ingenuity and hard work has failed. Dressage is the polar opposite of the "fast food" mentality that permeates the United States. It has become necessary to add an even lower level to the levels of dressage. This level is called Intro, where only the walk and trot are performed and there are no real dressage requirements. Most dressage riders in the United States are Intro or Training Level riders. Regardless, in theory, a rider advances in an organized manner "up the levels," labeled First through Fourth. Each level requires progressively more demanding execution of the movements of the horse and aids of the rider. From there, one does the FEI levels.

The Mysterious FEI

FEI stands for the *Fédération Equestre Internationale* and uses predominantly French terminology which is surprising for a sport dominated by the Germans. It is the mysterious international governing body of equestrian sports recognized by the International Olympic Committee. This is why it wields such power. The folks at FEI make the rules for real dressage, as well as for jumping, eventing, driving, vaulting, endurance riding and reining.

FEI is similar to the Nobel Prize and Academy Award committees in that the identity of its members is a closely guarded secret. This is to protect them from the occasional Intro and Training Level rider who "goes postal." The FEI levels in dressage are Prix St. Georges, Intermediaire I and II, and finally, the pinnacle—Grand Prix. The best thing about reaching the FEI levels is that the rider is finally allowed to wear a shadbelly, which is akin to a formal tuxedo coat with tails. Wearing a shadbelly, in addition to a tophat, is believed to be the point of this whole production.

The Generally Accepted Training Pyramid (GATP)

And so, dressage is laid out very clearly with concise goals to achieve at each level. If the levels are not enough to satisfy the most anal-retentive, there is also a Generally Accepted Training Pyramid

The Rider's Training Pyramid

(GATP), which outlines the sequential stages of a horse's training. To make this even more perfect, the GATP falls right in line with the levels of competition!

The GATP starts with rhythm and relaxation, moves to contact and *schwung*, then straightness and suppleness and, finally—the pinnacle—collection. The inclusion of *schwung* in the GATP was the FEI's way of gently introducing Americans to the new, exotic terminology of dressage. Unfortunately, many children cannot enjoy learning about the GATP because the word *schwung*, combined with rhythm and contact, does not pass America Online's child protection locks.

Nowhere in the GATP is there anything that corresponds with Intro and Training Level. This is because, as previously discussed, there are no actual dressage requirements at these levels. This is a somewhat inflammatory statement. Trainers and judges will argue that Intro and

Training Levels incorporate at least the bottom three rungs of the GATP. However, at the FEI levels, it is generally agreed that these trainers and judges are simply pandering to their clients.

The Battle to Revise the GATP: Classical vs. Competitive Dressage

Here is one interesting note to new dressage riders: FEI is currently embroiled in a minor controversy about revising the GATP. The Competitive School of Dressage is seeking to have collection removed from the GATP and replaced by extensions. The Classical School of Dressage is demanding that half halts supercede collection to reflect their overwhelming impact on the entire GATP. The sometimes stuffy Classical School also wants extensions removed entirely from all test requirements.

The Classical School has been boycotting dressage competitions for the past 500 years because of the requirement of extensions. So far, their efforts have fallen on deaf ears. A subcontroversy exists within the Competitive School regarding the definition of extensions and whether they truly are lengthenings.

In Conclusion

Debates such as these are quite common and have been going on for centuries in the dressage community. This will not matter to new dressage riders who are not doing any dressage at Intro and Training Levels. These riders will never actually perform any of the three contested dressage movements: collection, extensions and half halts. In fact, as dressage as a specialty does not begin until Third Level, all of the above and everything to follow is utterly meaningless to almost everyone in the United States who believse they are actually riding dressage.

Regardless, every great art form has its share of controversies and detractors, and dressage is no different. This should not blind people to the overwhelming greatness of dressage and the half halt. Clearly, dressage is the most enlightened type of equestrian expression and a worthwhile endeavor in all of its forms, except for perhaps Intro and Training Levels, where again, no dressage is actually performed.

> "Because dressage is a partnership between horse and rider, and the rider who does not study his horse's character, or who treats him like a machine, is the one least likely to succeed."
>
> **Jennie Loriston-Clarke, _The Complete Guide to Dressage_**

Poor Sassy, My Informal Introduction to Dressage

Learning dressage does begin innocently enough. As a former Hack Stable Queen, I was confident in my ability to "stick on" the most spirited of mounts. After the birth of my daughter Kat, my riding time dwindled to about nothing. When my daughter was a toddling 2 year old, however, I received a call from the former owner of the hack stable, who had retired from the business and was operating a small boarding farm. She still had a propensity for collecting really, really pretty horses who were, quite frankly, very "challenging" to ride. She asked if I'd be interested in, according to hack stable terminology, "riding down" a particularly spirited mare.

So, between working out child care arrangements and fitting this in around my job, I made time to work with another "outlaw" beauty, much like Midnight of my Hack Stable Queen years. Her name was Sassy. She was a Trakehner/Arabian-cross chestnut mare with lots of chrome. Pretty, oh yes! Sassy, I was informed, was a reject from a fancy hunter/jumper farm because of some soundness issues. She also was wicked, as only a chestnut mare can be. What is not to love here? Shades of The Black Stallion—a horse only I could ride!

Somewhere in Sassy's past, she had received some dressage training. I discovered while riding her that with creative manipulation of the reins, she would instantly go "round." Wow! It was awesome. I recognized this fancy, head-tucked-in look as the stuff really good riders could do. Hence, I must be a really good rider! Surely it had nothing to do with the rather harsh kimberwicke bit I rode her in. Hours I spent, trotting poor Sassy, so game, about the pitted, poorly maintained arena, see-sawing the reins to achieve my version of On the Bit.

This was much more fun than galloping cross country. I was suddenly captivated by trotting endless circles in the ring. I began throwing in my version of transitions until I could get her to go from trot to halt with a single jerk on the reins. The control and precision was intoxicating. I had heard about dressage, of course, but this was the first time I regarded it as anything less than deadly dull stuff. Interesting how my new fascination with doing circles in the ring coincided with having a toddler at home.

Yes, poor Sassy was my unofficial introduction to dressage. She is yet another horse who deserves a long overdue apology from me. ∎

A Moment of Reflection

"I actually rode a friend's Missouri Fox Trotter out on the trails not too long ago and he was so darn fun that it depressed me. When I went back to ride my guys I was so saddened by how much "work" it was that I thought about giving up dressage. I'm over it now. I love dressage. I love the learning and the feeling of those moments of perfect lightness and balance. I find it fulfilling and addicting but not necessarily fun."
Trakehner Addict, "Is Dressage Fun?" 6/24/03, UDBB

This is a good place to reflect on all of your past riding experiences. Take a snapshot in your mind and hold it close to your heart, for your perceptions regarding horseback riding are about to change forever.

If you are reading *Survival Guide*, it is probably too late for this moment of reflection, but try anyway. Remember those days when you could go on a trail ride and just enjoy yourself? Remember when you moseyed down the trail without staring intently at your horse's head to make sure he was "round"? When you didn't stress over the fact that he wasn't bending the right way—kick, kick, jerk, jerk, nag, nag? And then fret about whether you were asking too much or perhaps you were ruining the "training" by being too lenient?

You've consulted the books, and therefore are assured that trail riding is approved by the dressage masters—well at least some of them. That part is good. It is doubtful they engaged in trail riding at the Spanish Riding School of Vienna. However, most of us can content ourselves with slightly lesser standards, like Dr. Reiner Klimke. Dr. Klimke recommended trail riding in his books. Well, perhaps not trail riding per se, but at least he was often shown riding about in open spaces.

But does that mean you ask your horse to stay on the aids while moseying down the trail? Or should you go on the buckle? So, perhaps you compromise and do a little of both? Meanwhile all the beautiful cross-country scenery is passing you by, unnoticed, while your horse is rolling his eyes inwardly in disgust at the wiggling, waggling, unrelenting rider on his back. If your horse could talk, would he shout, "Lighten up, already!"?

Was there a time in your horsey past when you bought a saddle based on its affordability and perhaps color and never thought about tree width, twist, stirrup alignment and air ride panels? When the important thing was to have a really cool, colorful saddle pad? And when you had, at the most, two bits: The snaffle for ring work and the kimberwick for trail riding? Remember how simple life was back then?

Remember when you just enjoyed riding? Sure, your hands and seat were atrocious and your horse was stiff as a board with his nose poking in the air, but didn't you have fun? It's well worth the effort to look back on those days. No doubt you will see them through rose-colored glasses—just like when your parents talk about the days they walked nine miles to school barefoot in the snow, uphill both ways. Ah, the nostalgia of lost innocence!

Blissfull Ignorance

47

The Typical Dressage Rider: Middle Class, Middle-Age White Female

"If we are to raise ourselves up to higher levels of equestrian expression, we need to become constructively self-critical and develop a refined degree of self-control. An essential part of this lies in striving to put aside our ego. The earthly ego ever threatens to warp our ability to assess ourselves and our performance objectively. Only when our desire to learn is constantly tempered by modesty and a genuine interest in the horse's well-being, will we be on the path which leads to the blossoming of true horsemanship."

Erik Herbermann, *Dressage Formula*

Well, is that ever a weighty statement! In reading between the lines of Mr. Herbermann's statement (if you can), dressage is obviously an intellectual endeavor, which explains its attraction to middle class, middle-age white females (MCMAWF). It is particularly attractive to those with children because dressage engages the mind and the body in a complex synergy.

While the search for the perfect 20-meter circle may not appeal to a younger, more aggressive rider, it represents intoxicating appeal compared to folding yet another load of laundry or helping your 8-year-old son/daughter learn his or her multiplication tables. The pain of childbirth and the joys and tribulations of raising children have given essential preparation to these women to weather the travails of learning dressage. They have already exercised their self-critical skills at parent-teacher conferences and learned a high degree of self control when their child has spilled yet another glass of purple grape juice on the white carpet just prior to the PTA meeting being held there.

Today, dressage, for the most part, is the domain of MCMAWF who have switched from riding the more traditional American styles. One of the most appealing aspects of dressage, and one that attracts the MCMAWF, is that no jumping is involved. In addition, there is no mad galloping cross country and no livestock to rope, spear or otherwise wrangle.

Quite the opposite, dressage is a quiet, controlled sport contained within a rectangular 20-by-60-meter arena with lovely, soft footing to cushion against any stray mishaps. It is a sport in direct denial of the dangers of riding 1,200 pound animals hardwired with a fight-or-flight mechanism.

The propensity of the MCMAWF in dressage has given rise to more than a few snide remarks from those who ride in more vigorous equestrian sports. It has been rumored that dressage is for wimps. Take eventers, for example. They campaign in three separate phases: stadium jumping, cross country jumping and dressage.
It is a well-known fact in the horse world that eventers groan over the dressage portion of their sport. Imagine performing a staid walk, trot, ho-hum and canter yet another 20-meter circle on whippet-fit, straining-at-the-bit, long-legged jumpers while wide open spaces beckon.

On the surface it appears that, indeed, dressage is terribly dull to them. But the truth of the matter is they just can't do it and are anxious to move on to something easier: something like jumping a five-foot-high, three-foot-wide concrete wall with broken glass scattered on top and finished off with a 20-foot drop into a raging river. That is much easier than dressage.

One must scratch the surface of dressage only a bit to be frightened by its intricacy. In truth, the quest for the perfect 20-meter circle is an endeavor more challenging than completing the Rolex Kentucky Three Day Event cross country phase.

Hence, the attraction of dressage to the MCMAWF. No, these women are not wimps. They are supremely disciplined, critical connoisseurs of the perfect 20-meter circle—an accomplishment that frightens away even the seemingly bravest and boldest eventing riders.

Riding a Combined Test: No Fear!

It is a fact that I've actually participated in a dressage approved version of jumping called the "combined test." It gave me a minor celebrity among my dressage acquaintances: "You jumped?" While I made some attempts at false modesty, I was in fact bursting at the seams with pride. I actually ventured from yet another Intro Level test to try my hand at jumping. In a combined test, one does a dressage test and then jumps a course of fences. One of the wonderful things about this is that at my level—called Elementary—the jumps are only 18 inches to two feet high. How hard is that? Furthermore, the combined test is scored based on the dressage test! Then one merely has to clear the jumping portion, without time or pace constraints—points added on for refusals and rails down only. Easy, right?

As a MCMAWF with an utter devotion to dressage, I made a very important discovery: Most of the women I competed against were perhaps a decade younger than my 40 years. Most were mounted on huge Thoroughbreds or Thoroughbred crosses. These horses put in spectacular displays of bucking and various other high-spirited maneuvers while warming up, much to my dismay. While I consider my Andalusian, Capricho (better known as TFO, The Fabulous One), to be quite a hothead, he was a lamb compared to these powered-up jumping horses. It was scary, to say the least.

But, as a devotee to the perfect 20-meter circle, I was literally appalled at the event horse version of a dressage test. Don't get me wrong; I am highly critical of my skills at performing a perfect 20-meter circle, yet relative to these event horses, I felt like a Grand Prix rider. It's true! They can't do pure dressage! It was astounding to me how poorly they performed the 20-meter circle. Hello! The head is bent to the inside! I found their ignorance almost insulting the art form of dressage. Really, they all could have benefited from spending a couple hours reading Erik Herbermann's Dressage Formula.

I could also see them eyeing me suspiciously during the warmup. TFO trotted around with lovely cadence and his neck arched prettily, while these riders rode out some explosive bucks and seesawed the reins (gasp!). One rider even stopped and changed bridles. It took three people to hold her horse while she switched to "the big bit." I didn't ask what "the big bit" could possibly be. (Insert sniff of disdain here: What would Mr. Herbermann say about "the big bit," I wonder?) Needless to say, TFO and I were in first place by a wide margin after completing the dressage phase. And yes, it was yet another Intro Level test.

Now, that said, I have to admit that TFO did not perform very well in the jumping phase. While these big brutes were cantering boldly over these (little) jumps, my Capricho managed to refuse about half the jumps on course. We were eliminated. Yes, those event riders were exchanging satisfied looks then. Just as they suspected, snooty rider on fancy-pants horse couldn't really ride. I just bet they felt like handing me a copy of Jumping 101 for Stuck-Up Dressage Riders: How to Clear a Crossrail.

Ah well. But I had all those brave riders beat in the dressage phase! I took great consolation in that! The sad part was that I realized I was banished from a successful career as a combined training rider. Yes, back to the dressage arena for me and TFO. No easy escape from the rigors of learning dressage. If only he'd just jumped those fences!

A while later, TFO and I took some jumping lessons with a hunter/jumper trainer (on the sly, of course!). I wanted to find out what was wrong with TFO that he kept refusing jumps. The hunter/jumper trainer was very kind. She smiled gently and informed me there was nothing wrong with TFO. Quite the opposite, in his typical over-achieving way, TFO showed great form and style over fences. She did, however, have some recommendations for me. Apparently, I need to keep my eyes open and release my death grip on the reins when jumping a cross-rail! Easy for her to say. ■

CHAPTER TWO
The Journey Begins

The use of the word "journey" in describing your experiences with dressage is deliberate. While you are probably in a hurry to get to all the juicy stuff in this chapter, it is important to stop a moment to ponder the significance of the term "journey."

Simply defined, "journey" means a "trip." Doesn't that sound like fun? Like taking a trip to Cancun? We generally don't say, "My friends and I are taking a *journey* to Cancun to party it up over spring break." On the other hand, if we study biblical resources, the use of the word "journey" is quite common. This is because "journey" has a more solemn and profound implication than "trip." Moses didn't take a "trip" across the desert for 40 years—no, he was on a "journey." In the same spirit, we refer to a "dressage journey" not to a "dressage trip." It is important not to mistake this for something fun and carefree.

And while Moses' journey actually did end with the parting of the

Red Sea, you will not be so fortunate. There is no end to the dressage journey except for that ultimate end we try not to dwell on too morbidly. That would be death, *not* Grand Prix, for those who don't like riddles. So reflecting on the term "journey" is a useful exercise before reading onward. There might still be time to invest in that really fun trip to Cancun.

The Correct Way to Learn Dressage

Masters and Monks

> **"**It can actually be a hindrance if the applicant can already ride and has acquired a posture which does not suit the Spanish Riding School and can only with difficulty be altered.**"**
>
> **Requirements for entry as an éleve, Spanish Riding School of Vienna official Web site, *www.spanische-reitschule.com***

The best way to begin your journey is to explain the correct way to learn dressage. There is simply no other way to correctly learn correct dressage then to learn it the correct way. While that may sound like a somewhat confused statement, read it again. There are no shortcuts to correctly learning dressage. Masters have been riding dressage for centuries, and despite a few petty differences, they've all concluded there is only one way to learn it. At first, you will dismiss this as overkill. But before long you will find a new appreciation for what you are about to learn.

The only way to correctly learn dressage is to apprentice yourself to a master and spend the rest of your lifetime in his stable, under his daily guidance. Furthermore, you must never have swung a leg over a horse's back prior to working with the master. Not even a pony ride at the local fair. Even that slight experience will poison your ability to ever learn the correct way to ride dressage.

This is comparable to the type of commitment made by Buddhist monks. Think of Kwai Chang Cain in the 1970s television series, *Kung Fu*. Remember all the flashback scenes to his times as a child at the Shaolin monastery? Remember example after example of the self-sacrifice, subjugation of ego and just really painful stuff like picking up

Masters and Monks

the searing hot cauldron with his forearms? Remember how he referred to the monks as masters? Remember the blind Master Po, grasshopper? For those of you under age 40, now would be a good time to get on eBay and find a few copies of this truly great television series.

Cain turned out to be a really cool guy. He could kick some serious bad guy butt while spouting profound sayings about peace on earth and nonviolence and such. More importantly, his experiences learning to be a monk will give you an idea of what it takes to correctly ride dressage—in a suitably entertaining fashion. Cain, after all, was a renegade monk/master—kind of like a Grand Prix rider who decides to ride cutting horses.

The Apprentice—The First 30 Years

> **"**Years of experience show that out of four éleves a maximum of two stay on at the Institute and carry on with their training. The high reputation of the School and the quality of the work and performances mean that the selection process is tough.**"**
>
> **Dropout Quota, Spanish Riding School of Vienna official Web site, www.spanische-reitschule.com**

Those who wish to learn dressage correctly will become an apprentice to a master at a young age. Having never seen or ridden a horse before, it remains a mystery what attracted them to the master in the first place. The master will have the apprentice muck stalls and perform every lowly task available at the stable. Occasionally, the apprentice will be allowed to touch a horse and sometimes watch the master walk from the house to the barn. In this way, the apprentice learns the all important quality of humility, which is absolutely essential to correctly ride dressage.

After humility is established—a process that takes 10 to 12 years—the apprentice will eventually move up to leading horses. Leading a master's horse is fraught with difficulties, as one cannot pull back—ever—on a dressage horse. This is the stage where most of the apprentices are weeded out.

It works like this. Each spring, to determine the true worth of the apprentice, the master will hand the hopeful candidate his most spirited Lipizzaner stallion. The apprentice will then be asked to lead the stallion through a field of mares, most of whom are newly in season. If the apprentice, at any time, pulls back on the lead of the aroused, frothing stallion, he is dismissed from the master's stable—no exceptions. Many apprentices have been seriously injured in this tradition, even a few deaths have occurred over the centuries. Those few apprentices that survive this springtime ritual of "leading of the stallion" will then spend another 10 years mucking stalls so they relearn humility. ("When you can take the pebble from my hand, grasshopper," says Master Po to young Kwai Chang.)

The Lunge Line Rider—The Next Five Years

"The normal training as an éleve and involvement with a thorough training on the lunge in order to learn balance and posture is required in order to become a Rider."

The Training of the Rider, Spanish Riding School of Vienna official Web site, *www.spanische-reitschule.com*

It takes upward of 30 years before the apprentice is actually allowed to get on the back of a horse for the first time in his life. Fortunately, things start to move quickly from that point. The next

The *Student* is almost ready

stage is when the apprentice becomes a lunge line rider. Some masters feel this stage is too hurried and should be extended to a minimum of 10 years. However, since the lunge line rider is now approaching age 50, most masters will compromise here, given the average lifespan of the human being.

The lunge line rider has been suitably prepared for this new level. Despite his advanced age, he is fit from years of grueling barn work and has absolutely no ego to speak of. Furthermore, he has no wife, children, family or friends. In other words, he has no life whatsoever. To him, this lunge line work is quite fulfilling. The masters are so clever.

Round and round he goes on the lunge line, for hours a day, until he is dizzy, exhausted and befuddled. Although his apprenticeship was no piece of cake, here the master introduces him to new heights of agony. Year after year, our lunge line rider endures this torture, going around and around in tiny circles with no stirrups and no reins at all the gaits. It only stops when the lunge line rider falls from the horse in a limp puddle. Then the master unleashes a barrage of curses upon the semiconscious rider before calling it a day. Only in this way does the lunge line rider learn the correct seat to correctly ride dressage while maintaining his humility at the same time.

The Rider—The Last Decade

"The upkeep of the tradition of classical dressage and riding training is the duty of the riders and the senior riders. This training is done without text books and written orders and is passed down by word of mouth from generation to generation."

The Training of the Rider, Spanish Riding School of Vienna official Web site, www.spanische-reitschule.com

After surviving the years of apprenticeship and lunge line riding, the great moment arrives: He is now a rider. Finally, as he approaches the age of 60, he is able to pick up the reins of a horse for the very first time. His journey is about to begin. The masters, you see, know what they are doing. The rider has a perfect seat and will never pull back on the reins. He has humility. He has nothing better to do with his time.

Within a year, the rider is performing levade effortlessly on magnificent white Lipizzaner stallions. For him, dressage is simple. No longer is he a big loser and fits the FBI profile of a serial killer. Just like Kwai

Chang Cain in *Kung Fu*, now he is a really cool guy who can magically do really cool stuff on a horse while spouting profound sayings about half halts and world peace.

The rider will enjoy his position for the next 10 years or so, until he is too old and arthritic to ride anymore. He generally returns to the master's stable to oversee the apprentices mucking stalls from his wheelchair, a fitting end to his illustrious journey.

> **"***Today, the male riders are still carefully selected from within Austria itself and if found of sufficient talent and dedication, tutelage will start at 16 and end at 60. Riders have to be disciplined and highly committed, for the path ahead is not easy. If it takes 8 years to train a horse, it takes a lifetime to become a rider. Even the wisest of the Oberbereiters will never say they have finished learning.***"**
>
> **"Keeper of The Grail— The Spanish Riding School at a Time of Great Change" by Sylvia Loch, *www.classical-dressage.net***

[Authors Note: There is no mistake in referring to our apprentice/rider in the male form. In over 400 years, never once has the Spanish Riding School of Vienna accepted women éleves into their illustrious riding hall. Not once, ever. However, they do, once every four years, allow Sylvia Loch to write an article about them. We've come a long way baby!]

Betty Lester—A Blessing and a Curse!

Early on in my dressage journey, I have been privileged, or cursed perhaps, to meet a truly classical dressage trainer, Betty Lester. Betty, you see, is one of those few who truly understands the "correct way to learn dressage." When I first met Betty she was in her late 60s, and somewhat of an icon in my area. She rarely took on new students and her dressage abilities were whispered about in hushed and awed tones. Why, you might wonder?

Betty was training dressage back in the 1970s, when dressage was in its infancy in the United States. She worked for years under the tutelage of her mentor, German dressage master Fritz Stecken. The Stecken family was friends with the Klimke family in their home-town of Münster, Germany. Fritz, a bit older than young Klimke, gave Reiner his first riding lessons. In addition to being raised in a supremely accomplished equestrian family, Fritz trained under Otto Lörke and August Stäke, two great masters in their own right. Fritz himself was considered a master by the time he immigrated to United States after World War II.

Betty's instruction under Fritz Stecken was not all. She also trained with Bengt Ljundquist of Sweden and Franz Rockawansky of the Spanish Riding School. Another important teacher was Paul Keck, a master instructor and international rider from the Royal Hungarian Academy. And finally, Betty worked for with Dr. H. M. Van Shaik for two summers in Cavendish, Vermont. Dr. Van Shaik was from the Spanish Riding School and represented the Netherlands many times in Olympic competition.

Betty counted the late Bertalan de Nemethy among her friends and remembers when Olympian Lendon Gray was a kid, just starting out. She remains close friends with Marjory Haines Gill, another Fritz Stecken studen, and the first woman dressage rider to represent the United States in the Olympics. I hope you are suitably impressed and in awe with these credentials. I know I am! Meeting Betty, watching her ride, watching her teach and even taking a few treasured lessons myself, profoundly impacted my dressage journey. She would be the yardstick by which I would measure every trainer who came before or after her.

But, it's like the cliché "not knowing what you don't know." I was convinced that Betty held the classical standard like a banner, but I was woefully unable to interpret what exactly all that meant. I would forever look at my future trainers with a suspicious eye, wondering if they were upholding the "correct" methods and if Betty would approve.

I'll never forget the time that Betty rode Gus, my second (but not last) dressage horse. I had practically thrown myself at her feet, groveling for help.

Pathetic! Betty finally took mercy on me because she really loves horses and felt terribly sorry for poor Gus. Imagine this, if you will. Betty, in her late 60s, has some serious back and neck injuries. She's a tiny thing as well, only about five feet tall. Betty insists on riding properly dressed in white breeches and tall boots. As my request (OK—desperate plea!) came during a riding lesson, she went back to her house to change into her riding attire before riding Gus. I was quite impressed and taken aback with that level of detail given my Hack Stable Queen background.

I was breathless with anticipation to see what miracle she'd perform on my 16.1-hand, one-quarter draft horse—the definition of "heavy." Gus was one of the kindest souls on earth, so I was not worried for her safety as she climbed aboard. This was also the first time I'd seen Betty ride. Well! If you open up one of your classical dressage books and study pictures of the late, great masters, sitting absolutely correctly, upright yet supple, with the perfect shoulder/hip/heel alignment, that was Betty.

So there she was, mounted on my Gus. She proceeded to walk him around the indoor arena. I couldn't detect any undo exertion on her part, but she quickly frowned and muttered under her breath, "Oh my! Yes, oh dear, he is quite difficult to lighten." she said. I was really puzzled at this point. After all, she was just walking. How could she know? But I could see at great level of concentration flowing between the two of them. For about five minutes she walked and halted Gus and performed a few leg yields. I could never get Gus to leg yield.

Her beautiful position never changed through these quiet exercises. There was no huffing, puffing, yanking and cranking or cursing and swearing–the typical reaction by all who have ridden Gus. It was all quiet and concentrated.

Gus' entire persona changed before my very eyes. He seemed to lift himself up from his shoulders, his head and neck proudly arched. His eyes took on a soft and glowing light. He looked, well, he looked utterly beautiful. After a few more moments, Betty asked Gus to move off at the trot. He literally floated. I wanted to cry. Watching Betty transform my somewhat ungainly but modestly talented Gus into such a beautiful and happy creature–in about 10-minutes–would forever crush my confidence.

I made a vow to myself when I sold Gus and bought TFO: No matter what difficulties I'd encounter with TFO during our journey, no one would ever ride him but me. I never wanted TFO to know what it should really be like because I will be incapable of that level of skill in my lifetime. This, actually, is a principle of horsemanship that Betty advocates–obviously for good reason. I suspect somewhere in Betty's past, Fritz Stecken mounted her favorite horse and transformed him before her eyes. I've maintained my vow, and I still own TFO. In this you can see why, then, knowing Betty has been a curse.

Yes, witnessing Betty's level of skill crushed me. But on the upside, I received a most precious gift from Betty. It was through Betty that my daughter was introduced to Chico, her Nokota horse. Much to my disappointment, my only daughter had been indifferent to horses until she was captivated by Chico's adorable personality. Betty, along with her friend Marjory Gill, is a supporter of the Nokota Horse Conservancy. Marjory Gill actually owns six of these rare horses. I now appreciate what attracted these supremely accomplished horsewomen to this breed. While you may never see a Nokota performing Grand Prix at the World Equestrian Games, you cannot imagine a horse with more grit and a bigger heart than a Nokota.

So, I may never ride even to First Level, but I have something so much more special. Watching my daughter's love for horses blossom through her relationship with her Nokota, Chico, has been an unanticipated gift. The time I now spend riding with my daughter and the special bond that has created between us, is something I cherish beyond words.

In this, you see, knowing Betty Lester has been a blessing without end. ■

How You Will be Learning Dressage

"Every interested rider has to bear in mind that dressage means training, not exhibiting. Horse and rider must have a good foundation. The rider must sit correctly so that he is not interfering with the horse's balance. The horse must move forward naturally and briskly, remaining balanced and relaxed, in the walk, trot, and canter. With such a foundation, many horses and riders can reach the highest degree of horsemanship."
Fritz Stecken, *Training the Horse and Rider*

There is a remarkable difference between how to correctly learn dressage versus how you, the typical dressage rider in the United States, the middle class, middle-aged white female, will be learning dressage. You, for obvious reasons, will be unable to apprentice yourself to a master for 50 or 60 years. Even if you hope to, as discussed, the masters don't accept women riders.

As the average newcomer to dressage, you generally do not, at first, comprehend the intensity of the journey you are embarking upon. You made the decision to try your hand at dressage because all your former friends are doing it, and you have no one left to ride with.

You have noticed the profound change in your former carefree riding companions, and at first, you think it's a bad thing. No longer are invitations to go trail riding being accepted by your dressage friends. You get some mumbled excuse and the phone is slammed down in your ear. You're puzzled; were they crying? When you bump into them at the tack store, your former friends are in intense consultation with the saddle fitter or combing over the latest Mylar bits looking for the one that's been newly approved for dressage competitions. Your friendly "hello" is acknowledged with a distracted and somewhat disdaining nod as you head over to check out the new line of colorful saddle pads. How snotty they've become, you think.

Gradually, though, you have no one left to ride with, and you're getting seriously bored with trail riding alone. Then the day will come when you get bucked off your usually mellow Quarter Horse gelding while out on a trail ride because he's tired of hacking out alone as well. Now that you are getting older, it will take you a month to recover from the fall. When you fully recover, you find you have little interest in trail riding and think dressage might be really cool. You have noticed that nicely cushioned arena and the lack of jumps, and realize the time as come. You miss your old friends and, what the heck, let's give dressage a try. How hard can it be, after all?

Selecting Your First (But Not Last) Trainer

"If we don't know anyone, the other thing to consider is looking for is a trainer who has a foreign license (like a Bereiter or Reitlehrer). Then you at least know you're getting someone with a certain level of knowledge/training- and not someone who learned to ride last week, thought teaching would be fun and decided to hang out a shingle. Unfortunately, if they smile a lot, they manage to fool enough people long enough to stay reasonably busy. Sooooooooo sad.**"**

horseaddict, "Selecting an instructor," 12/4/03, UDBB

Selecting your first (but not last) dressage trainer is one of the most significant steps you will take in your journey, only you don't realize it yet. It will be this trainer who will launch you correctly—or incorrectly—along the path. The quality of this trainer is dependent upon many things, but herein lies the first major pitfall you will encounter in your journey. While dressage is growing by leaps and bounds, there are many loud and strident complaints about the dearth of qualified dressage instructors.

To understand the difficulty of selecting the correct trainer, it is helpful to take a look at the German model. The Germans are the reigning rulers of dressage. You may disregard those who will argue this comment; they are just bitter. The reason Germans are preeminent in dressage is because, number one, Germany is located next to Austria and the Spanish Riding School of Vienna. That was just lucky. The second reason is because of the nature of the German people; they are utterly anal-retentive.

Who else could scientifically engineer one of the most enduringly popular breeds of dogs—the German Shepherd—in less than 100 years? In their rigorous, nationalistic way, the Germans ruthlessly managed the breeding and registration of this breed. For example, only eight puppies may be registered in a litter. What happens if 12 puppies are born? The extra puppies are "culled"—that's what happens. What is "culled"? I think you know.

The Germans manage the raising and training of dressage riders and horses in the same harsh, but effective manner, under the auspices of the German Equestrian Federation (FN). Germans learn to ride at the various branches of the German riding school. If they graduate only eight riders from their program, and 12 had been enrolled, what do you suppose happens to the other four? I think you know.

Now, try to fit that model of horsemanship into the American culture and you can easily see why it doesn't work. People for the Ethical Treatment of Animals (PETA) and the United Nations Commission on Human Rights would be on our case in a skinny minute. Obviously, being the world's only superpower does have its drawbacks: Everyone is ready to jump on our case for the slightest infraction of human and animal rights! Geez!

It is helpful to take a look at what has happened to German Shepherds transplanted to the United States. Hip dysplasia sums it up. Americans took this very same breed and created a dog so deformed that most are crippled with hip dysplasia by age 2. How did we achieve this brilliant piece of genetic misengineering? In the American dog show ring, unlike the German show ring, it's all about the look. There is no culling, and there is no performance testing. Not surprisingly, most German Shepherds used in police work are imported from Germany.

Much the same has happened with dressage. The guiding organization of dressage in the United States is the United States Dressage Federation (USDF), founded in 1973. As a frame of reference, the Spanish Riding School was formed in 1572. Those 401 years has given the Spanish Riding School a significant advantage, no doubt. USDF has a thankless task for sure. Because of all the do-gooders, they are not

Pferdewirchaftmeister Pferdewirchaftmeister Pferdewirchaftmeister furdywurchamister Pferdewirchaftmeister

allowed to cull trainers, riders or horses, except under the most extreme of circumstances. This is a democracy, after all, and as such, anyone is allowed to participate. How does one set high standards under those parameters?

So what all this technical stuff mean for you as you go about selecting your first (but not last) trainer? Do trainers get hip dysplasia, you may be wondering? Of course not! It simply means that here in the United States, there is no uniform way of selecting a trainer. It's a crapshoot out there.

Eventually you will understand why all your friends get excited when the *Pferdewirchaftsmeister* (head guy certified by the FN) from Germany is giving a clinic in your area. A *Pferdewirchaftsmeister* is even better than a *bereiter* (professional rider certified by the FN) and the *reitlehrer* (training guy certified by the FN). All these guys have passed the culling process, you see.

The First Lesson to be Learned

"Pulling on the reins implies the use of a backward action of the hands which is always, under any circumstances, fatal."

Henry Wynmalen, Dressage: *A Study of the Finer Points of Riding*

Teaching you the first lesson to be learned is why your first trainer will not be your last trainer. It doesn't matter if your first trainer is a really great trainer. As you begin dressage you will be quickly overwhelmed by how difficult it is. Given the lack of the all-important culling process, you will inevitably become convinced that your first (but not last) trainer must be wrong. It's only human nature.

You see, the very first lesson you will learn in dressage is that everything that goes wrong is the rider's fault. This is different from any other form of riding you've done. Before dressage, you generally thought of the horse as either getting or not getting the message. Sure, you needed to perfect a few skills, like posting to the trot, but in these other disciplines you were never considered intrinsically incorrect from the get go.

Depending on the effectiveness of your trainer, this point must be driven home like a stake through your idealistic heart. Your seat, your hands, your leg position—all together—contribute to driving your poor horse crazy.

Conversely, everything that is good and right about your riding is directly the result of the innate generosity of your horse for overcoming your many obvious riding flaws. In the case of a new dressage rider, if the horse happens to "get it," it was purely an accident.

This is the first, yet the most difficult lesson to absorb. It is a subtle thing; you think you have accepted it, only to find fatal arrogance will creep back into your training at various stages. In fact, you can anticipate teetering between soaring conceit and utter despair throughout your journey.

As one starts dressage lessons, and this message becomes apparent, you are at the beginning of watching your self-esteem crumble. It is not that this lesson is necessarily incorrect or meant to be cruel, it's simply that dressage, as discussed, is a lifelong journey and, by definition, after a lifetime, you still won't get it right. This is why to correctly learn dressage one goes to the Spanish Riding School of Vienna.

If it's any consolation, your first (but not last) trainer will not be surprised when you eventually abandon her. You see, this trainer is the one with unenviable task of introducing you to dressage. Whether good, bad or indifferent, this trainer's task is a difficult and thankless one. Unfortunately, given the chaotic state of dressage training in the United States, you will no doubt go through many trainers before truly accepting the first truth of dressage: It's all your fault. ("When you can take the pebble from my hand, grasshopper." says Master Po to Kwai Chang Cain.)

To think you gave up trail riding for this punishment?

In Search of On the Bit

"A horse 'held in shape' by his rider is only posturing in a seemingly correct outline, usually for the benefit of the inexperienced observers.**"**

Charles de Kunffy, Dressage World, Famous Quotes,
www.dressageworld.com

And why, you might ask, is this first lesson to be learned so difficult? The reason is that you fundamentally misunderstand the concept of dressage, which is the development of self-carriage in the horse through the perfect seat of the rider. You will be sidetracked from that objective because you will be desperately seeking On the Bit. Deep down, in your heart of hearts, all you really, *really* want is to get your horse to arch his head and neck—to be On the Bit—just like in all the pictures.

This is called On the Bit riding and has nothing whatsoever to do with dressage. Beginning dressage riders are obsessed with On the Bit riding. You believe that is what dressage is all about.

Done correctly, we ride our horse from back to front. This means we engage the hindquarters, through our seat and legs, and bring the energy up into the head and neck, whereby at some magical point the horse will arch his neck in the classic dressage frame. The hands merely regulate the energy generated from the hind end. That is riding back to front. Simple. Ha!

The reality is somewhat different for struggling new dressage riders. We can't see what's going on behind us; we can only obsess endlessly

Finally on the bit after all these years!

over what is in front. Therefore it is simply irresistible to use our hands to get our horse On the Bit. Our rides become a grueling torment, where we yank and pull and kick, all to get our horses to arch their head and neck. It doesn't work. Hence, our self esteem continues its downward slide.

Your First (But Not Last) Horse

> **"**The quick answer—and I know this is cheating on a tough question—is don't put green on green. You're a beginner in dressage. Your horse is a beginner in dressage. In that situation, every beginner ruins their first horse.**"**
>
> **SmithsonLM "And yet another question about contact," 8/28/03, UDBB**

The reason your first dressage horse will not be your last dressage horse is the same reason why your first trainer is not your last trainer. You are referred to as "green on green"—neither of you has a clue!

Again, it is helpful to look at the German model here. Beginning dressage riders in Germany are started on appropriately trained school horses. In the United States, there is no such thing as appropriately trained school horses.

As Americans, we tend to think of ourselves as the independent type and quite clever to boot. We don't need to start on some old, moth-eaten school horse when we already own a perfectly fine horse. All we are really trying to do is get our horse On the Bit. What's the big deal? So, we think, we will take a few lessons on our perfectly fine nondressage horse, and learn On the Bit.

It quickly becomes apparent, however, that our perfectly fine non-dressage horse just isn't getting this On the Bit thing. It becomes very discouraging to take lesson after lesson after lesson, and still, no On the Bit. "Stupid horse," you think, because you haven't fully absorbed the "First Lesson to be Learned." Please re-read that section.

What's worse, your first (but not last) trainer will get on your horse at any point, and get your stupid horse On the Bit, while explaining, in unexplainable jargon, that On the Bit isn't really the true objective of dressage and that you still have not absorbed the "First Lesson to be Learned." This trainer will throw out obscure terms like "lightness" and "thoroughness" and "*schwung*!" You won't be listening. You are too busy staring at your horse's head to ascertain if he's On the Bit. And you yank and crank and kick and so on.

Soon, you are despairing of your first (but not last) horse. You are becoming suitably humiliated during every lesson and eventually come to the decision that you need to get a horse more appropriate for your purposes—in other words—a horse *trained* to go On the Bit.

It is incredibly bittersweet to part with your first (but not last) horse. He was a great guy, just not capable of On the Bit. Your first (but not last) horse, on the other hand, is relieved to be changing hands. At this point, he is the finest shape of his lifetime. He has been schooled five days a week and is in fighting trim. His feet are perfectly balanced, his back has been massaged and his teeth are in perfect order. Never in his life has he had so much fuss and attention yet still been considered a huge disappointment to his rider. He will happily go off to the hunter/jumper barn with a new, nondressage rider who is in awe of his skill of bending into corners and getting the correct lead and doesn't care in the least about On the Bit. ❏

CHAPTER THREE
Aids on Your Journey

Quickly, the depth of your inability to ride is starting to glimmer in the forefront of your conscious mind. Being a reasonably bright and resourceful person, you will realize the need to educate yourself beyond your weekly lessons with your first (but not last) trainer.

Fortunately, there is a veritable wealth of books and videos available to you. Even more fortunately, most are available online, so all that is needed is the time surfing the Internet with your credit card in hand. As you are now spending an enormous amount of time on the Internet, you will eventually come across the dressage Web sites, forums and bulletin boards. You will be totally hooked. Your time spent reading, watching videos and participating on Internet sites will eventually eclipse your actual time spent riding by a ratio of 100 to one.

The Books

"_The problem with reading a lot of books is that you only get out of them what you are ready, so to speak, to learn. You can read a lot of advanced technique stuff, but until you are mentally and physically ready for it, it doesn't sink in, or worse, confuses you. Welcome to the journey!_**"**

AndalusianMom, "Need suggestions for useful reading material," 12/3/03, UDBB

And there they are: Books and more books: _Dressage Formula, Dressage in Harmony, Introduction to Dressage, Dressage Explained, Cross-Training Your Horse_ and its companion, _More Cross-Training, Dressage From A to X_ and so on. These are the easy books. Eventually you'll move on the _The Gymnasium of the Horse_ and look for a translation of Xenophon's masterpiece _The Art of Horsemanship_ written in 360 B.C. (no kidding!).

You will find these books to be very solemn and earnest. Dressage, you see, is a serious endeavor. It is a blending of technique with artistry. You will read about its comparisons to figure skating, ballet, the martial arts and even ballroom dancing. Of course, none of these admirable pursuits are partnered with an animal, thereby making dressage even more illustrious when mastered. You will spend a lot of time leafing through these books and mostly looking at the really cool pictures. It is informative to note that very few people are smiling in these pictures. They are not doing this for fun nor, if you look closely, does it look like they are having fun. This is a warning you should take to heart.

You will no doubt order your first few books from amazon.com and wait breathlessly for their arrival. You even considered shipping them FedEx Next Day, before the additional cost dissuaded you. When it finally arrives, you eagerly wrestle with the tightly wrapped brown box. After an hour or two, you finally release your prize from its packaging. Though slightly winded from your exertions, at last you are able to happily ensconce yourself for a few hours of pure dressage reading. Really, it's like sitting down with the ultimate mystery book. The answer is in there! This might be an innovative marketing tip for publishers of dressage books—cross-reference them with the mystery selections. It's rather surprising no one has thought of this before.

But reading your dressage books is really just a microcosm of your entire dressage journey. Generally, the foreword and prologue will be the liveliest reading of the entire book. (Note the subconscious parallel to Intro and Training Level in that statement.) Here the author will delve into his/her background and offer an outline of their general dressage philosophy, which you will, of course, eagerly approve of.

But two things will start to seep in as you bravely progress to chapter one. First of all, you will be immersed in the minutia of every step and footfall that a horse makes. It's, well, honestly, quite dull reading. You will go cross eyed as the aids to the walk are explained in fantastical detail. You will reread "aids to the walk"—all 25 sections—three or four times before giving up and moving on to chapter two, "Aids to the Trot." "Aids to the Trot" is even more complex than "Aids to the Walk." Soon you'll skip to just scanning the titles of each chapter—Chapter 26—"Aids for *Lügenstrassen*,"—and quickly move on. "What's a *lügenstrassen?*" you wonder with a puzzled shake of your head. Before long, you'll be rereading the foreword and flipping through to look at all the cool pictures.

The second thing that starts to filter in as you read "Chapter One: Aids to the Walk," is the increasingly harsh admonishments about *incorrectly* performing the aids to the walk. Rather quickly, nagging guilt forms in the back of your mind. You didn't realize how significant the aids to the walk were, as you are still early on in your journey. You begin to recognize yourself in these examples of improper timing of the aids. It starts to dawn on you that *you* are the one responsible for destroying the quality of your horse's walk and, indeed, his entire dressage career because you know you have jerked back on the reins and thereby destroyed your horse's innate sensitivity to the aids.

Still, you think, maybe this is just relevant at the walk and turn to "Chapter Two: Aids to the Trot." Here, perhaps, you will find something *good* about your riding ability. But it only gets steadily worse. Whatever sins you've committed at the walk are compounded a thousand fold at the trot. There is so much to go wrong, and you just had *no* idea you were *so* awful. At this point you're afraid to turn to "Chapter Three: Aids to the Canter," Subsection XXVIII, "Getting the Left Lead Canter." Compared to dressage authors, Irish Catholic nuns are amateurs in making one feel sinful in the face of good intentions.

Reading & Riding

[Author's Note: Author from family of mostly Irish descent with many fallen-away Catholics relatives. So, please be cautioned at Author's bias: Fallen-away Irish Catholic female tends to feel guilty easily.]

As with all things to do with dressage, you will put your first (or second, but not last) dressage book away on the shelf and order a different dressage book, only to find it contains pretty much the same variation of excruciating minutia and stern warnings regarding rider errors. You are sure, if you buy enough books, you will eventually find the correct answers and be relieved of ever-burgeoning guilt. In this way, you see, your dressage library will expand to breathtaking proportions in no time at all.

Another thing to keep in mind is that in the really good dressage books, the pictures are all black-and-white photos of older gentlemen, preferably in military garb. The really, really, *really* good dressage books have no pictures. They may, however, include some hieroglyphics from cave drawings, a sign of a truly great book.

And an important note of caution: There are a few "feel-good, positive-thinking" dressage books. As you become more sophisticated, you'll be embarrassed to have these in your library. They contain brightly colored pictures, snappy text and smiling people. The smiling people are a dead giveaway. This is like "Dressage for Dummies." No need to throw them away, simply tuck them to very back of your library. If a dressage acquaintance should spot them, claim it was a Christmas present from a well-intentioned but misguided relative. Despite your mutual sniffs of disdain, be aware your dressage friend has that very same book in her library.

The Videos

Along with your mushrooming collection of dressage books, you will also start accumulating a tasteful selection of dressage videos. Videos are somewhat tacky compared to the awe-inspiring knowledge available in the books. And because you're a *serious* dressage rider, you don't want to be dismissed as a fly by night. So growing your collection of videos must be undertaken cautiously.

It is best to go with a series. There are several series out there. The best offer Volumes 1 through 18, from "Selecting Your Young Prospect" to "Grand Prix." At first you will be frustrated, because nowhere in Volumes 1 through 18 will you find the video about Intro and Training Levels. This, you see, is because these series are done by masters. Masters never talk about or even acknowledge the existence of Intro and Training Levels. You will find this out only after buying Volumes 1 through 3.

Volume 1 features magnificent, young warmbloods, buffed and polished, being ridden On the Bit and performing lengthenings (extensions?) and half passes. They perform these effortlessly. These are the "Young Prospects." In Volume 2, you will be captivated by these same magnificent warmbloods, a week later, performing one-tempi changes and canter pirouettes. By Volume 3, they are discussing the beginnings of the piaffe-passage tour. Nowhere is there Volume 1½—Intro and Training Levels.

Market analysis has shown that sales drop off dramatically between Volumes 4 to 16 and then resurge for Volumes 17 and 18. These would be the ultimate two videos—Grand Prix (Volume 17) and Grand Prix Freestyle (Volume 18). Now this is what we're talking about! You will be riveted to the images of these magnificent creatures at the height of their glory. Yes, these are the same stunning warmbloods seen in Volume 1, one year later. After watching Volumes 17 and 18, you'll rarely watch Volumes 1 through 3 again. They will only be dusted off every year or so when you are in the process of buying yet another dressage horse.

One of the best uses of the videos, particularly Volumes 17 and 18, is after a particularly bad lesson. It is truly a balm to the soul to watch the masters dance effortlessly across the arena on these brilliant horses after your confidence has been tattered to shreds trying to get the left lead canter. Despite your temporary delusions that you were truly attempting a counter-canter, you, your trainer and your horse really know the deep-down truth: You still can't get the correct lead and move out of Intro into Training Level.

So, you will come home, despairing at ever mastering dressage. You'll pour a glass of merlot, dim the lights and pop Volume 18 into your VCR. You will mute the volume, play your favorite music and relax and feel rejuvenated by these images of dancing horses. Soon this will be you!

So, you see, the videos, tastefully collected, are a wonderful comple-ment to your dressage library and, in many ways, more uplifting, espe-cially after a particularly bad day. This is not the time you want to open up your collector's edition of de la Guérinière's masterpiece. At times like this, we simply need the images to flow effortlessly from our television screen. There is no need to be ashamed of this; we all deserve an occasional break from the intensity of learning dressage.

[Authors Note: To date, the dressage video series has not been digi-tally remastered and presented as a Gold Edition DVD. It is only a matter of time, not to worry. The production companies are merely waiting to unload their leftover inventory of Volumes Four through 16, circa 1982.]

The Nokota Horses and The Truth About Horsemanship

Relative to most serious dressage riders, my dressage library would be termed "barely adequate" (much like my riding skills), and I have only a handful of videos. Being very cost conscious, the rate at which I acquired books and videos diminished when I tapped into the "free" Internet dressage resources. Of course, just so you don't think less of me, I do boast books by both Klimke and Podhajsky. My all-time favorite dressage video is a collection of famous Grand Prix horses performing freestyles. I love turning the volume down and watching Reiner Klimke and his champion horse, Alerich, perform a freestyle to the music of my choice: "Bad to the Bone" by George Thorogood and the Delaware Destroyers. It's awesome, really, you should try it.

I have other videos in my collection, unrelated to dressage, but which have very much affected my dressage journey. These videos document the story of the wild Nokota horses and their hard-scrabble life in the Badlands of North Dakota. The life and times of

Nokotas are about as far removed from the rarified world of dressage as one can imagine. Who could have guessed that my family's involvement with these horses would give me yet new insight and further burst my ego regarding the riding of dressage and the truth about horsemanship?

You see, about the time we acquired Chico, our Nokota horse, for my daughter Kat, I was immersed in horrible angst with my second (but not last) dressage horse, Gus. My frustration and obsession with dressage had probably (hopefully) reached its peak.

After getting Chico, I eagerly began my version of dressage training with him. At this point, my daughter had a total of only four riding lessons. That pretty much qualifies as a complete beginner. And Chico was still fairly green. So you can see the urgent need to apply my "training" skills to get Chico up to snuff.

He was a remarkably good sport about it. In fact, I found him remarkable in many ways. A century of scrambling about the extreme terrain of the Little Missouri Badlands made for a breed of horse as agile as a mountain goat. Combine this natural athleticism with years of outwitting predators both natural and manmade, and you have quite an amazingly bright, balanced and light horse. The bottom line is that riding a Nokota is like being aboard an all-terrain vehicle with brains. No half halts required. I kid you not!

Riding Chico was incredibly easy after bouncing around on Gus, my big Thoroughbred/Percheron-cross gelding. What a remarkable contrast Chico's gaits were smooth, his size fit me well and, all in all, I begged my daughter to let me have him. She refused, point-blank. Smart kid! It was no coincidence that shortly after getting Chico, I sold Gus and got my Andalusian, TFO, who is, guess what, the same size, color and type as Chico, but has a much better mane and tail. The only downside is that Andalusians, unlike Nokotas, do require half halts.

So everyone is happy, right? Wrong! I have been forced to watch day-in and day-out my daughter's remarkable ease of hand and seat as she tools about effortlessly on her little gray Nokota. How unfair is that? She has not invested years of sweat and tears to achieve her seemingly effortless connection with her pony. Oh no! That would be her envious mother.

I still can't quite figure out how Kat achieves this connection. Perhaps she inherited natural talent from me? Doubtful. The best I can determine, Kat's ability comes from her close bond and absolute trust in Chico, which allows her to ride without fear or constraint. Perhaps her very lack of riding experience prior to getting Chico was actually beneficial? She had no preconceived notions about how complicated riding can be. Ah well. Thankfully, as a mother, I beam with pride over Kat's accomplishment. As a rider, well, I envy her innocence and pure joy in her riding. It's so not complicated for Kat.

Of course, that is not the only lesson learned from my experience with the Nokotas. It gets worse—much worse. I've had the opportunity to get to know the founders of the Nokota Horse Conservancy. Brothers Leo and Frank Kuntz are fourth generation ranchers and horsemen from North Dakota. North Dakota is a universe removed from my firmly East Coast equestrian experience.

Needless to say, these guys know nothing about dressage. They do not own a dressage library nor boast a shelf full of dressage videos. They ride—you probably guessed this—Western. But I tried not to hold their ignorance of dressage against them. After all, they have spent their entire adult lives doing good work by saving the Nokotas. They have been otherwise occupied from developing a keen knowledge of the half halt and the shoulder-in.

There was one particular conversation I had with Leo Kuntz. The talk segued from the Nokotas into riding styles and techniques. Leo talked about the importance of having, as he put it, "a good hand" on a horse. He said no matter how good the seat, without a good hand the rider was not a horseman. I will swear that Leo Kuntz has never read Gustav Steinbrecht's The Gymnasium of the Horse although Mr. Steinbrecht dwells on this very concept in the very first pages of his classic dressage tome.

It got worse. Leo went on to talk about the two ways to ride bareback. Apparently, when growing up on a ranch in North Dakota, riding horses is a given. As a safety measure their parents never let them ride in saddles. It seems there was too much danger of getting a foot stuck in the stirrup or being otherwise unable to bail out quickly. Leo described to me the various methods for riding bareback. There is the wrong way—which is gripping on with the legs. And there is the right way—which is using balance without gripping with the legs. After this conversation I idly flipped through the pages of Henry Wynmalen's Dressage: A Study of the Finer Points of Riding, paying particular attention to his chapter on riding in balance and the importance of "letting go" or not gripping when riding dressage.

Wisely, during this conversation with Leo, I made affirming noises and kept my mouth shut regarding my sophisticated dressage techniques. How could I have known that a Western rider could have such a firm grasp on these classical dressage principles? There was obviously nothing of value I could contribute to in this conversation with a true horseman, despite his woeful lack of dressage training.

So there you have it: The truth about horsemanship. I don't have personal experience regarding this, but I can proudly say I've witnessed it firsthand with *my daughter* and with these guys from North Dakota. This how the Nokota horses have enriched *my* life and further burst *my* ego. ∎

The Internet

The Internet is truly the greatest resource available to sidetrack dressage riders from actually riding dressage. Fortunately, there is a trade-off. Your newfound computer ability is probably the single most useful skill you'll achieve out of your dressage journey. Finally, you are motivated to overcome your ineptitude regarding modern technology. The Internet, you see, will enhance and enlighten your dressage journey in a myriad of ways.

It will start fairly simply when you set up your premium account with amazon.com. Here you will purchase many of your new dressage books and videos. After all, it's unlikely that Gustav Steinbrecht's *The Gymnasium of the Horse* (published 1885) will be readily available at your local bookstore or on the bestseller book rack at your supermarket. Buying your books from amazon.com or bn.com also saves time—time you need to read these profound texts.

In addition, many tack stores offer online shopping. This is of enormous benefit. Since you've started dressage, you need to purchase a new and different bit every week. In fact, it's quite startling, compared to your pre-dressage riding experience. You used to own two bits. Now you have at least 123 bits of various sizes, makes and models, and none of them work. You are still looking for the magical On the Bit bit. Imagine how difficult your task would be to find the On the Bit bit if you had to actually drive to one of three tack stores in the nation that distribute this "must-have" item?

And consider how much horse buying and selling has been impacted by the Internet. Even a decade ago, it was unlikely you'd purchase a horse outside of your reasonable driving distance. And even that was a time-consuming process of receiving and reviewing gobs of photos and sales videos through snail mail. Now, with national "horse for sale" Web sites like agdirect.com and dreamhorse.com, combined with e-mail and digital scanning, the entire country has opened up to prospective buyers and sellers. Since you will be purchasing a new dressage horse every year or so, the Internet has made your life so much easier. In addition, looking at horse for sale Web sites is a great way to pass the time fantasizing between horses.

The Ultimate: Dressage Online

"It would be nice for every rider to ride with a [Karl] Mikolka, or a [Charles] DeKunffy or a WAZ [Walter Zettl]. But that is not reality. Most riders struggle just to afford the board bill, and if they are lucky, one lesson a week. This is not in any shape or form a classical school-

ing where riders only ride schoolmasters and only ride under the watchful eye of their instructor. So these posts on the Internet, while not a perfect world, at least give some of these folk an opportunity that would otherwise not be possible."

Katherine, "The value of free advice," 1/3/04, UDBB

These are just a few ways the Internet has enhanced your dressage journey. But it gets even better. Eventually you will stumble upon the dressage forums, bulletin boards and discussion sites and, at last, you have found nirvana! Much like Internet dating services, the stigma attached to participating in these outlets is starting to fade. A few of these forums have gained formidable reputations and boast internationally acclaimed dressage riders and trainers among their members.

Here, at last, you have found the ultimate outlet for all the pent-up frustrations accumulated on your journey. These forums, you see, are online discourses among folks who ride, or try to ride, or want to ride, or have ridden dressage. You will find these sites and quickly register as a member so you can observe the discussions. At first you are a "lurker"—someone who reads, but does not participate. The length of time it takes you to go from "lurker" to "participant" depends upon your personal self-esteem issues. You will be fascinated and bemused by the variety and depth of these discussions.

But lo and behold, these folks have the same issues and questions that you do. You are not alone! Some even have *answers* to some of your questions! And they actually care! No longer will you have to pester your spouse, children or coworkers and watch their eyes glaze over as you recount your latest dressage dilemma or infrequent triumph. You might have noticed that your youngsters hate to have the latest rerun of "Rugrats" interrupted to hear about your dressage lesson.

It's hard to believe they cannot comprehend the significance of weighting your left seat bone when asking for the upward transition into the canter and at the same time releasing the inside rein by $5\frac{1}{2}$ of an inch, whereby your horse lifted into the first stride of a lofty upward canter on the correct lead at the very moment you moved your inside leg back by 9/12 of an inch and captured the resultant energy waves into your outside rein, and at that exact moment you brought the outside leg forward by 6/12 of an inch, thereby freeing the inside shoulder and then, the next stride of canter you. ... What is *not* riveting about that?

Best of all, online you are "anonymous." When you eventually stop lurking and start participating, you can speak as freely as you'd like because your identity is a secret. Word to the wise here: The horse world is a still a small world, even online. Don't be surprised to find the woman you can't stand at the barn—the one you just posted about at length on the forum—is really forum member "Dressage Witch." Keeping this in mind will save you many embarrassing moments, and you won't need to switch boarding barns so often. Careful what you say!

The down side to dressage online is that you hardly ever see your horse anymore. Much of the free time you used to spend at the barn is now spent discussing your latest On the Bit dilemma on the forum when you're not searching online for the latest On the Bit bit. After the first year or two of struggling mightily to achieve On the Bit, you learned some coping skills and have diversified your efforts. It's so much easier, after all, to sit in front of the computer screen bemoaning your horse's lack of dressage suitability than to actually ride. Indeed, dressage online has revolutionized this art form for struggling dressage riders.

Straight from the horse's e-mail

The Ultimate Dressage Bulletin Board and Riding Deep

It should come as no surprise after studying many of the quotes in Survival Guide that my Internet home away from home is the Ultimate Dressage Bulletin Board (UDBB.) Back when I had my first (but not last) dressage horse, Chad, I spent a lot of time online researching the prices of Grand Prix Arabians. Obviously, I was still incredibly naïve at that point. I happened by accident upon the USDF discussion forum. Timing is everything, and for once I had it.

In 1999, USDF's rather cumbersome site was struggling with the infamous Y2K debacle. It was believed to be the only victim of that much-anticipated event. By the new millennium, the USDF site unofficially morphed into the UDBB under the guidance of Mark Susol, an opinionated, yet dedicated dressage afi-cionado. Mark (also known as the Boss Hoss) is now the head babysitter of a forum that boasts more than 1500 mostly female, angst-filled dressage riders from around the world. Lucky guy! Rumor has it that the Boss Hoss is currently working on his own book, Forum Moderator Survival Guide. Look for it soon!

Yes, what a monster he created. UDBB brings together a diverse group of dressage fanciers from around the world, ranging from complete novices to such illustrious characters as Lendon Gray and Walter Zettl (forever known by his online handle, WAZ). Other illustrious big names who have "popped in" to marvel at the UDBB spirited debates are Robert Dover and Charles deKunffy.

Some of the characters on the UDBB have taken on their own "celebrity." They are generally heavy posters; every post on the board is tallied. These folks offer knowledgeable advice, constructive criticism and often much needed sympathy. At the top of the UDBB heap are the online trainers. The grande dame is galopp, who in real life is dressage judge Paula Kierkegaard. And no, she did not misspell her name. "Galopp" is actually the German word for "canter." This should give you an idea of the depth of knowledge some of these trainers boast.

Other online trainers we turn to for advice and solace are the wise "horseperson," the kindly "MsKreuz," the down-to-earth Kathy Johnson, and the philosophical Katherine. We can always count on these ladies to offer intelligent answers to all those burning On the Bit questions. Yes, all these individuals selflessly devote themselves to bringing us "into the light"!

Other very popular posters include Lynne Flaherty, also known as TSandM. TSandM is priceless, as you can see for yourself in the foreword of Survival

Guide. She is an openly struggling amateur dressage rider who rides quite well and has a truly stunning technical grasp of the intricacies of this "art." We can always count on TSandM to give insightful yet sympathetic critiques of our various angst-filled issues. TSandM's posting tally is more than 5,000 and counting.

Likewise, the gentle Lynne S, a student of the above-mentioned "horseperson," is an esteemed and knowledgeable poster always ready to help. Monica S, Zoeneen and SmithsonLM are others who are guaranteed to offer interesting perspectives on our dressage dilemmas. There are many, many other colorful characters that populate the UDBB. Truly, it's better and more addicting than any soap opera you've ever indulged in.

Survival Guide was born on UDBB. In a moment of insanity, I posted my original short story, written for my own amusement (and therapy). The response was overwhelming, and I was encouraged to develop Survival Guide into a book. Trust me: If I were able to address every issue suggested by the board, this book would rival The Gymnasium of the Horse in breadth and scope.

And, so, there is only one true way to repay the support of my fellow UDBB members. The time has come and the place is here. Drum roll please .... We are going to talk about "deep." No, this is not the solution to the puzzling Watergate mystery, who is Deep Throat. And no, I'm not speaking about a perverted sexual practice.

Please! Even though you're disappointed, hello, this is a dressage book! So pull your mind out of the gutter and let's get serious! Simply stated, "deep" is the most divisive topic ever discussed on the UDBB.

Deep riding or rollkur is a controversial training technique first seen with Nicole Uphoff and her Olympic horse, Rembrandt, and then popularized by highly successful Olympic riders like Anky van Grunsven and Isabell Werth. These ladies pack a pretty significant punch when it comes to successful dressage riding. As a struggling Training Level rider, I admit I'm not qualified to explain "deep." I can only then give you my impression, from a novice's perspective.

The horse is ridden by the rider with his head held unrelentingly "down and round," rather than the classical up-and-open position. In its most extreme form, the rollkur, the horse's neck is forced very low, so that his nose is literally held to his chest while employing lateral flexions. In addition to using the undeniable leverage of the double bridle, tie-downs, such as draw reins, are often utilized to enforce this position. While the use of tie-downs like draw reins is not advocated by these Olympic ladies, rumors abound about their use at the less visible levels.

The horse is ridden vigorously at all the gaits in this position. It looks horrifying. The amount of time he is held in this position is subject to debate—estimates vary from a few moments to an entire schooling session. You might wonder at the logic behind "deep" or rollkur? Apparently, when the rollkur is complete, the horse is supposedly freed up in his back and is much more "submissive" to the aids. The rollkur is strictly a training method, and no such movement appears in any dressage test.

I asked my 12-year-old daughter to give me her impression of a picture of Anky van Grunsven riding a horse in a rollkur. My daughter has only been riding

about two years now. After she rolled her eyes at yet another strange request from her mother, she studied the picture for a moment and said, "I don't like it." "Why", I asked. "Because the head is all wrong, his nose is, like, touching his chest, and his back legs are wrong—they're hanging out behind him. The rider has a really nice position though."(Kat is available for horsemanship clinics if anyone is interested.) Keep in mind, though, Anky van Grunsven has won multiple Olympic gold medals in dressage. What could she possibly know that Kat and I do not?

The horses bred for upper-level dressage are truly "superhorses" with incredible power, size and scope. Couple that tremendous athletic ability with superb fitness and high spirits (or a bad day) and being "submissive" to the aids can be considered a life-and-death proposition. These elite horses don't have the benefit of a couple days turn-out to roll about and "be a horse." And, after all, we're talking about "big business" at these levels.

Is "deep" the utmost cruelty inflicted upon a horse? Or is it a fantastic breakthrough in the art of dressage? I don't know. I'm still trying to get On the Bit. I mean, I feel bad about pulling back on the reins. Is my version of On the Bit as horrible as "deep"? For what it's worth, the Olympic caliber riders using rollkur advise against amateurs "attempting this at home."

Horses have been on the short end of a lop-sided arrangement with humans since the beginning of time. If my livelihood, or very safety, were at stake, would I use rollkur? Yes, I probably would. Let's face it: If horses were given a choice, do you think they'd want to do dressage, or would they rather loaf about the pasture with their buddies and eat lots of grass?

I do believe the answer can always be found by looking into the eyes of the horse. Whether we can do anything about the answer we find there is another story entirely. Frankly, a horse in rollkur does not exhibit a soft, happy eye. Quite the opposite, in my humble opinion. The beauty of forums like UDBB is that issues like rollkur, right or wrong, are brought into the light of day, to be examined and dissected. In the end, it is the horse and our horsemanship that benefit from these heated debates.

That is all I can say about "deep," the most controversial subject to ever arise on UDBB—my Internet home away from home. ■

CHAPTER FOUR
Dressage Movements

Now that we have explored the aids for our journey, it is time to turn our attention to the actual dressage movements. This will necessarily be the shortest chapter of *Survival Guide*, given the lack of technical expertise of the author. However, I would be remiss not to touch upon this subject. Absolutely every book about dressage discusses gaits and the dressage movements. And so, therefore, shall we.

The Gaits

"*In dressage, which aims to lead to the most advanced forms of riding, this purity of gait is of absolute importance, and must not be overlooked, either by the rider, the judge, or the instructor.***"**
Henry Wynmalen, Dressage: *A Study of the Finer Points of Riding*

This seems simple enough. The horse has three gaits to consider: the walk, trot and canter. The gallop, which is the most fun gait, is not used in dressage, except by accident, and therefore will be left unexplored. Yes, this should be pretty basic stuff but certainly, by now, you've realized that nothing is simple or clear cut in dressage. We understand that the goal of dressage is to improve on what nature gave—or didn't give—each horse.

It is here, particularly, where your library of books will be most enlightening. As discussed, in these books, each gait is broken down into excruciating detail. Each and every footfall is examined with ferocity. Gaits within gaits are scrutinized. Yes, I'm afraid so—there are levels to achieve within each of the gaits called working, medium, extended and collected. Other "gaits within gaits" include lengthening, which seems to be exactly like extensions, but are, in fact, different. No one can seem to explain why this is. Don't be upset if you can't tell "gaits within gaits" apart in the pictures and diagrams. Remember, this is a much nuanced art form, and you are not Michelangelo.

The Walk

"If the horse's walk is naturally bad, training, no matter how good, will ever make it great. A great natural walk can, however, be ruined by bad training."
John Winnett, Dressage as Art in Competition

The walk, you see, should be marching, but not rushed and certainly not too slow. It is a four-beat gait. It is proclaimed that the walk is the most difficult gait to "train" and/or improve with dressage and the easiest to ruin. It is therefore of urgent importance to buy a horse blessed with the ideal walk. As the walk is the most difficult gait to improve and so easy to ruin, it seems strange that fledgling dressage riders must spend so much time riding at the walk, and it is judged so critically at shows.

Let's elaborate. When showing at the lower levels, particularly the all-important Intro and Training where most of us reside, the walk, and specifically the free walk, is given a double score, called a coefficient. That's right, as unfair as it may seem, the free walk—walking on a loose rein—is considered vitally important to show the progress and training of the horse. Though this may seem to defy logic, it is not for us to question the experts. This problem may be sidestepped, therefore, by purchasing a horse that has a good walk.

The walk will hopefully show "overstriding." This concept remains somewhat obscure to the naked eye, but apparently it means that the hoofprint of the hind should come ahead of the hoofprint of the front hoof. Got that? If you happen to be passing a newly dragged dressage arena, don't be surprised to see trainer and student squatting down and peering intently at the Perma-Flex to examine the hoofprints. Don't mistake them for practicing paleontologists on the trail of a new dinosaur discovery. They are merely checking for overstriding at the walk. This way, they will determine if the rider needs to buy a new horse or not. You will become used to this as time goes on.

[Author's Note: My young twin sons, Alex and Nick, are in the last stages of their dinosaur obsession. I promised them I'd fit dinosaurs somewhere in *Survival Guide*. It was either dinosaurs, *Sponge Bob Square Pants*, or *Yu-Gi-Oh*. Surprisingly, Alex and Nick find the subject of horses and dressage quite dull. They can't understand why Mommy is giggling maniacally while writing this.]

The Trot

> "*If a rider possesses skill in the art of riding, the quality of a mediocre trot can be improved, especially through the gymnasticizing of the hindquarters, because this improves impulsion in the horse.*"
>
> **Walter Zettl, *Dressage in Harmony***

Next we have the trot, which is a two-beat gait. As the horse trots, his legs move in diagonal pairs. Fledgling dressage riders will spend a lot of time exploring this gait. The invention of posting (standing and sitting strategically to the rhythm of the movement) has helped riders worldwide survive this bouncy, awkward pace, thereby making it one of the most accessible of all the horse's gaits.

Overstriding

In dressage—and of course this won't surprise you—it is preferable to sit the trot.

One would assume then, that the ideal trot would be smooth and comfy to sit, like the lovely "jog" of the Western-trained horses. Well, duh! Of course not! The ideal trot in a dressage horse is a BIG trot. *Really* BIG! HUGE is definitely preferable! In fact, the bigger, bouncier and more uncomfortable the trot of the dressage horse, the more prized the horse is!

Especially desirable is the toe-flipping trot—the exclusive domain of warmbloods—where the front legs actually smack the horse in the nose on an alternating basis. Now that's BIG! The toe-flipping trot has also been referred to, in a sometimes derogatory tone, as the "expensive trot," generally by members of the Classical School. It has something to do with deep-rooted controversy over extensions versus collection and, unfortunately, beyond the scope of this chapter.

Now would be a good time to page through the books in your dressage library and look at pictures of those Grand Prix horses. Turn to the section on gaits. Find the one where the Olympic rider is performing a spectacular extended trot (lengthening?) across the diagonal. You know the one I'm talking about. Look and marvel at how BIG that trot is!

Note that the Olympic rider is *not* posting. Look at the expression on the rider's face: You can tell the rider is a lot of pain! The more distressed the face, the better the quality of the trot. The scores given for the trot are in direct proportion with the pain of sitting the trot. So, this is why a dressage horse with a BIG trot is such a prized show animal. And you can certainly appreciate why Olympic-caliber riders are so revered for their stoicism in the face of great pain. This is why many Olympic riders are men. It is not, as initially suspected, a discriminatory thing. Men obviously have the advantage of suffering the most pain while sitting the trot. Truly, their agony defies the imagination.

There are other ways to confirm the quality of the trot in a dressage horse, though the pain factor in sitting the trot remains the most straightforward. One is called diagonal advanced placement (DAP). If you've never heard of DAP, consider this a gift. You can really impress your dressage friends with this one.

Agony of the seat

Although it is generally accepted that the trot is a two-beat gait, in fact the best trot—one that has positive DAP—is a *four-beat* gait. Confused? It's really quite simple. This is because ideally the hind foot will strike ahead of the front foot by up to, but not to exceed, 40 milliseconds, thereby in reality making it a four-beat, not a two-beat, trot. That's right, you heard correctly, milliseconds!

DAP, positive or negative, is not visible to the naked eye. Not to worry! Determining your horse's DAP is quite simple. Hire a professional videographer to tape you and your horse performing the sitting trot. Then watch the film in slow motion using a specially calibrated stop watch to calculate the milliseconds between each footfall. Soon your horse's DAP will become apparent. It is especially helpful if you enlist the aid of a Ph.D. from some famous Swedish university to be by your side the first several times to make all this clear.

Calculating DAP

If you are on a budget and can't afford a Ph.D.'s assistance, watch the film in slow motion and look closely at your facial expressions for grimaces of pain. That works, too, in calculating positive or negative DAP. Remember, the more pain the better.

If your horse does have negative DAP, there is some consolation. Unlike the walk, which can't be improved and you've no doubt already ruined, you can make significant improvement in the trot through dressage training. So don't despair if your horse has a comfortable, smooth trot to start. It can be fixed! With hard work and determination, you will find the quality of that trot improves steadily, until one day, you will be (hopefully) groaning in pain in the extended trot (lengthening?) across the diagonal.

The Canter

"There is no general agreement amongst authorities as to the precise system of aids most suitable to obtain a strike-off at the canter. The question is somewhat complex."

Henry Wynmalen, Dressage: A Study of the Finer Points of Riding

The canter is a three-beat gait. With careful study, you will come to know exactly which leg is off the ground at any given moment in the canter sequence. It is essential to understand this timing to learn how to ride the canter correctly. For some reason, the canter and the walk are closely associated. It is therefore important that you buy a dressage horse with a good canter. Like the walk, it is difficult to improve upon. Unlike the walk, it can be improved *somewhat*. What a relief! No doubt you think we are talking in circles here, but one merely consults the books to see this is true in regard to the canter. And besides, circles are the essence of dressage anyway, so this makes some sort of sense in a spiritual way.

The canter is ideally a lofty, slow moving, three-beat movement. Most beginning dressage riders make the mistake of fixating on the inside front leg as the leading leg, hence, getting the correct lead. This is, of course, wrong. The *most* important leg in getting the correct canter is the outside hind.

Keep in mind, there is a perverse beauty to dressage, whereby everything you thought was "right" is really "wrong." Remembering this simple premise will make your journey much smoother. So of course, you are not surprised to learn that the outside hind, not the inside fore, is the most important leg in the canter. See that?

Unfortunately, it is much more difficult to determine what the outside hind leg is doing compared to the inside fore. You can't simply glance down and see for yourself. After a while you will break yourself of that habit because you will develop a feel for where each leg is through your seat and your eventual psychic connection with your horse. In the meantime, the time spent looking down to check the lead can be used to ascertain if your horse is On the Bit.

Summary of the Gaits

So, let's take a moment to recap what we've learned about the gaits, and in particular the gaits of a good dressage horse. The walk is the most difficult to improve upon, is easiest to ruin and, therefore, one of the most important gaits when being judged. The trot is ideally as uncomfortable as possible. The good news is that even the smoothest, most comfortable trot can be improved to make it uncomfortable, and thus competitive. Also in dressage we sit rather than post to the trot, to increase our pain factor and, again, our competitiveness. The canter, like the walk, is difficult, though not impossible, to improve. And forget about the inside leading leg: You're wrong about that.

So the essence of dressage is to improve the gaits of any horse, except for the walk and the canter. The one remaining gait that can be influenced is the trot. We can make the trot uncomfortable, which is probably why we all want to learn this captivating yet confusing discipline.

The Half Halt

> **"**The half halt is the most important concept in all of riding, because it calls the horse to a perfect state of balance, harmony and attention.**"**
>
> **Robert Dover, Three-time Olympic and World Equestrian Games bronze medalist in dressage as quoted in More Cross-Training by Jane Savoie**

Sigh. The half halt is perhaps *the* most important aid in any riding discipline. While in most cases, we have seen whatever is generally accepted as correct in other disciplines is wrong in dressage, this is one case where what you thought was correct really is "correct." This still makes sense, given our understanding of the perversity of dressage, because the half halt is almost impossible to do correctly. This is why, in this case, it is correct in dressage. Got that?

The half halt is the essential tool required to rebalance your horse. As you have (hopefully) figured out by now, dressage is all about achieving balance with your horse. Therefore, one uses the half halt constantly—nonstop, in fact—at all gaits, gaits within gaits, through transitions, in the lateral movements, and leading your horse from his stall to his pasture (the in-hand half halt).

Piaffe, is really, just one giant half halt. If you've been fortunate enough to see a piaffe performed, you will notice the horse is trotting in place with a distressed look on his face and lots of frantic tail swishing. This is because the rider is giving the horse a series of mega half halts—the ultimate expression of "Stop, No I Mean Go, No I Mean Stop, No I Mean Go, etc." Truly gifted riders make this mega half halt seem like dancing but, in most variations, it looks like someone driving a manual transmission car for the first time.

To explain how to correctly execute a half halt, it will be necessary for you to turn, once again, to your library of books. There you will finds reams of information of about how to do a half halt. Yes, chapter upon chapter, devoted entirely to the half halt. For those who are visual learners there are even two videos by Jane Savoie, *The Half-Halt Demystified, Parts 1 and 2*! Half halt has such a mystique that even the publisher of this book is named after it. Its very name achieves instant "cache" with equestrians everywhere who understand the half halt is something only the most sophisticated riders can perform correctly.

So, here we can only explain how most of us give a half halt, which is, of course, the incorrect way, but simple in its execution. This is how you will respond when your first, second or third (but not last) trainer screams at you from across the arena: "Give a half halt, NOW!" You will jerk back sharply on the reins. Simple, but wrong! The correct half halt is given through the seat and back first. Only after the half halt is given through the seat and back, do you jerk back sharply on the reins.

It takes years and years to really understand this concept. Unfortunately, the correct half halt is *essential* to training your horse. This is one of dressage's dirty, little secrets. The inability of most riders to properly execute the half halt is why most of us remain mired in Intro and Training Levels for decades. It's not that your horse lacks dressage suitability, and it's not because your trainer is not a good trainer. It is because you can't do a correct half halt.

The problem is that you believe you are actually performing a half halt when you jerk back sharply on the reins. You believe this because your first, second or third (but not last) trainer keeps telling you to half halt. You surmise, therefore, that you are giving a half halt but, in reality, you are not. This explains the many times your first, second, or third (but not last) trainer crumbles onto the Perma-Flex and pounds her fists in utter frustration and despair, mumbling "half halt, half halt, half halt" in a demented chant. This is because you still haven't actually performed the half halt. Understand?

Transitions

Transitions, as the name implies, are those fleeting moments in time when you go from one gait to another gait. They are divided into upward and downward categories. For example, as you ask your horse to go from walk to trot by jabbing him with your spurs and smacking him with the whip while simultaneously pulling back on the reins, you are asking for an upward transition. Conversely, going from the trot back to the walk—by pulling back sharply on the reins while jabbing your horse with your spurs and smacking him with your whip—is known as a downward transition.

It is generally accepted that downward transitions are more difficult than upward transitions. This is because it is harder to coordinate your aids in the timing of the downward transition. While the pulling back on the reins is fairly instinctive, it's difficult to get the concept of spurring and whipping your horse at the same time; it seems to defy logic. However, in dressage, one strives for an "upward" downward transition at all times. This is why the use of the spur and the whip is crucial, combined with pulling back on the reins. This way the horse is going "up" while going "down."

In the upward transition, the use of the spur and the whip seems appropriate, while pulling back on the reins does not. However, pulling back on the reins is essential to achieving On the Bit, and therefore is forever ingrained in your subconscious mind. Struggling dressage riders always pull back on the reins, regardless of whatever is being asked of the horse.

On closer examination of the upward and downward transitions, one begins to understand that the transitions are ridden very much like the half halt. Indeed, the halt halt, which is being applied constantly to the horse (as discussed previously), is needed to perform correct transitions, because the transition is nothing but a half halt. The transitions, however, lack the mystique of the half halt. To the best of my knowledge, there are no videos devoted exclusively to the transitions.

Here is a puzzling thing about transitions: When you consult your library of books, you will be hard pressed to find pictures and diagrams of the actual moment the various transitions occur. That would be the actual moment in time where the horse's legs seem to get tangled up and lose their clear two, three, or four-beat rhythm. This is strange as the footfall sequence of every gait and gaits within gaits is explained with such detail. But nowhere have I found the sequence of footfalls when the thundering canter drops into the strung-out trot. A simple explanation for this is that transitions generally aren't that attractive, even when performed by advanced riders.

Lateral Movements: Shoulder-In and Beyond

"I learned to leg yield within the first year of riding dressage, but until I could get the horse truly connected and control the haunches and shoulders separately, the leg yield was not really correct. That's been in the last year or two. (I've been doing dressage for 14 years.)"
TSandM, "Rider Learning Curve—never ending," 11/30/03, UDBB

The lateral movements are the really cool stuff in dressage and pretty much beyond the scope of this book. It is hard to explain what you don't know, after all. Therefore, the important thing to understand here is that the lateral movements are of critical significance in training your dressage horse. More bluntly, if you can't perform lateral movements correctly, you will never leave the ranks of Intro and Training Levels.

Rider position is of crucial importance in any of the lateral movements, which is one of the reasons why most dressage riders cannot perform them. The elusive half halt is another vital element. And most importantly, the horse must be trained by a Grand Prix rider in these movements so that the horse has a 50/50 chance of figuring out what your fumbling aids mean. These factors combined are why most of us never learn lateral movements nor leave the ranks of Intro and Training Levels.

However, depending on the quality of your instruction up to this point, you will have been introduced to lateral movements in some form or another. Most likely you will have attempted the leg yield. The leg yield is a really cool movement where your horse goes sideways, while also going forward, across the arena. Hopefully his legs will be crossing. He is *not*, however, bent in the direction he is moving. That would be a half pass or perhaps the full pass. Neck bend is crucial in performing lateral movements. It is unlikely you will ever acquire enough skill to change your horse's neck bend and achieve the half or full pass.

Interestingly, the leg yield is somewhat controversial. Apparently, it should only be practiced for a limited amount of time, or you will risk ruining a horse's dressage career. This is why it is one of the first lateral movements taught to beginning dressage riders. If you should become remotely competent at the leg yield, it will have to be summarily dismissed from your repertoire.

The good news is that most beginning dressage riders achieve only what is known as the neck-bent, shoulder-leading, non-leg-crossing stagger across the arena. It is safe to practice this lateral movement at both the walk and the trot for an unlimited amount of time without risking your horse's future in dressage.

Another lateral movement that is practiced as a grotesque caricature of its true form is the shoulder-in. While not as exciting as the beginner's version of the leg yield, shoulder-in is one of those mysterious yet vital movements essential to performing correct dressage. This is clear because of the controversy that surrounds the shoulder-in. Much acrimonious debate revolves around the three-track shoulder-in versus the four-track shoulder-in. Don't expect to comprehend the difference between the two. Again, this is something way outside the scope of your understanding.

Just be aware that the difference divides dressage into two camps—the German School and the Other School. The Other School's most famous representative is the somewhat mysterious Nuño Oliveira. By consulting your books, you will eventually come across Oliveira. It will just take a while. Be advised that the information contained about the Other School is shocking, relative to what we believe as the normally accepted classical dressage principles, as in the Spanish Riding School of Vienna.

The German School performs the three-track shoulder-in. The Other School performs the four-track shoulder-in. Masters from both schools have engaged in violent debates over who is correct. To date, no clear winner has been determined, despite having the best minds on the job for centuries. (No one is quite sure how long Oliveira lived, but it seems at least from the mid-16th Century to the end of the 20th Century.) Here in the United States, the German School dominates, but practitioners of the Other School are still available to make us doubt everything we've learned from the German School.

It is therefore important for beginning dressage riders to ascertain which school their first, second, or third (but not last) trainer belongs to and side with her. When you become embittered with your trainer, you will at one point or another switch to a trainer from the Other School. It won't help you learn dressage, but it will give you certain vindictive pleasure when your last trainer finds out you switched sides. A word of advice here is to avoid burning bridges because you will eventually switch sides several times during the course of your dressage journey.

Rest assured, your version of both the three-track shoulder-in and the four-track shoulder-in will look pretty much the same. It is called the "neck bend." You will perform this by twisting your body awkwardly while pulling back and *sideways* on the reins, while at the same time using the spur and the whip to achieve forward motion. The only difference between any of the lateral movements from the half halt is that you make sure your horse's head is bent at an uncomfortable angle. Got that?

This all you need to know about the lateral movements, shoulder-in and beyond.

Riding with the Other School and Getting a Lobotomy!

The more astute here have probably surmised that my tangent regarding the German School and the Other School comes from personal experience. Admittedly, I'm an impatient type, and my frustration with learning dressage led me, rather quickly, to go exploring for an easier way to achieve harmony with my horse. It is not easy to find practitioners from the Other School, but if you should come across one, don't let the opportunity slip past you. If you thought you were confused before, you will be stunned at the depths of despair still unexplored!

The Other School loves the Iberian breeds such as Andalusians and Lusitanos. So, upon getting TFO, and being much wiser, I was duly motivated to enroll in a clinic with a practitioner of the Other School based on the pictures advertising her clinic. She wore a strange side-ways hat and rode a white Lusitano stallion. Perfect!

I took several intriguing clinics from this trainer before giving up in despair. There were things that were so cool like the idea of having "stillness" in your body. Kind of like a Zen thing. Sounds silly, but it never occurred to me that all *my* attempts at giving the aids might result in a great deal of useless "noise" to my horse. The bonus is that if you're still, you don't have to worry about the timing and coordination of the aids. Aha! I could be onto something here!

But with the good always comes the bad. The Other School just adores the lateral movements. The more the better! And they are particularly fond of the four-track shoulder-in. Ugh! Now, to be fair, they love the other lateral movements as well, but unfortunately one must be proficient at the four-track shoulder-in before moving on. Hence, all I ever learned was how to do the four-track neck-bend/body twist.

I think I could be in line for some sort of award for performing the worst—hideous really—four-track shoulder-in. Poor TFO! With the utmost concentration, I'd point his nose to the fence at a 45-degree angle and then twist my body at some ungodly angle while yanking his head one way while his body turned the other way. We'd stagger along like this for awhile. Then I'd stop, with much relief to both of us, pat him and go back to 20-meter circles. Trust me; the three-track neck bend practiced by the German School is much easier!

There are other things that are truly shocking about the Other School. I was told—I swear—that there was no need for the old "inside leg to outside rein" deal! How about that? Keep in mind, most Intro and Training Level riders have no clue how to actually ride "inside leg to outside rein" but nonetheless, we've been thoroughly indoctrinated to its significance.

Indeed, the Other School goes further. Some practitioners from the Other School believe that the horse should go on a loose rein! They argue that a horse can't truly be in self-carriage if his head is constantly cranked in. While there is some logic there, it still flies in the face of the German School as practiced by Intro and Training Level riders. Can you imagine being On the Bit on a loose rein? Not likely!

Their biggest proof is offered in demonstrations of the Iberian horses clearly On the Bit on a loose rein in the bullfighting arena. The best option here is to sidetrack the debate by objecting stridently to the inherent cruelty of bullfighting. The best defense is always a good offense and, in this case, it works like a charm to distract people from the issue of loose rein versus tight rein.

I was really game to attempt this loose rein, sitting still, Zen kind of riding advocated by the Other

School but, as it turned out, to do it correctly, you had to master the four-track shoulder-in. I can't explain why, but apparently this is so. I eventually came to the decision to stop going to clinics by this practitioner of the Other School. It all becamel too much for me.

I also seriously thought about getting a lobotomy to erase all dressage knowledge from my mind so I could once again enjoy trail riding. After all, what's a little drooling among friends? I consulted with my insurance provider, but alas, there was no coverage for this kind of procedure. The state of insurance coverage in this country is just criminal. We can only hope that as dressage becomes more and more popular, the request for this type of operation will eventually gain acceptance. ■

CHAPTER FIVE
Tools of the Trade

At this point in *Survival Guide*, one hopes you now have a clear understanding of the development of dressage in the United States and the all-important "correct way to learn dressage." Hopefully (doubtfully?) you understand by now that it is impossible for you to ever learn correct dressage. Ideally, you should be further concerned after delving into the "Aids on Your Journey" chapter and reviewing the puzzling "Dressage Movements: Shoulder-In and Beyond." You may have been sidetracked investigating DAP, for instance. Could this be true, you question? Yes, as you've ascertained, it's all true!

However, you are either the eternal optimist or completely obsessed at this point. So, you will still turn to this scholarly chapter in hopes of finding some redeeming quality—something to keep alive your fervent ambition to correctly ride dressage. So let us start this all-important chapter with yet another gift (like DAP). Here are your *Cliffs Notes* on the origins of dressage and the development of the tools of the trade.

A word of warning: While our journey has thus far been a (hopefully) humorous one, the time for fun and games is over. In this chapter, *Survival Guide* reaches above the standards of mere "fluff" non fiction. Given the serious nature of dressage riders, we knew this turning point was inevitable. After all, how much laughter can we stand? Yes, the comic tour-de-force is over and it's time to get serious. I'm sure you are relieved!

The Origins of Dressage— 460 B.C. to 1885 A.D.

> **"***Almost every existing field of endeavor has expanded over the centuries. Classical equitation, however, still finds its fundamental roots in past centuries. It is no wonder ... the horse held such importance in people's lives and drew the best minds of the time. ... The old masters were kind enough to pass on their legacies and thoughts, almost all of which are still sound today!***"**
>
> **John Winnett, *Dressage as Art in Competition***

This may seem an odd place to discuss the beginnings of dressage. But many tools of the trade have evolved over centuries. By understanding the history of dressage, you will be able to intelligently assess the merit of any particular tool, depending on where it originated. This won't help you ride dressage correctly, but perhaps it will help put your growing pains in perspective. The folks who developed dressage have been bickering over the details for centuries. Why should you be any different?

In some ways, dressage can be compared to classical music. It seems that all the great concertos and operas were written by the end of the 1800s. Why? During the first half of the 20th Century, we were distracted with two world wars. Then, of course, television was invented and permanently sucked the creative juices out of our brains.

Regardless, the great musical masters—Beethoven, Bach, Mozart and the rest—had already explored every note of music and exposed every simple emotion. The grand orchestras of today, for the most part, merely interpret the works of these great masters. And for the vast majority, classical music is a real bore, especially when compared to MTV. Like classical music, everything you need to know about dressage has already been discovered. And like classical music, most people find dressage boring, believe it or not!

Just as music is comprised of a vast assortment of instruments, dressage also has its own accompaniments. Today we use the same equipment—the bits, the bridles, the saddles, the whips, the spurs and the vast array of tie-downs—that were used by the great masters. Achieving On the Bit obviously is not something done while riding bareback with a halter and two lead ropes.

Keep in mind there have been many superb masters throughout history, but only the ones who bothered to write down their philosophies are remembered. The others have faded away into the mists of legend. The common thread throughout all the great works of the masters is submission and/or obedience of the horse. How this all-important quality is achieved accounts for some of the brutality associated with origins of dressage. This art form—dancing with your horse—has quite the dark side. So, here are your *Cliffs Notes*:

Xenophon (430–355 B.C.)

> "*If you desire to handle a good war-horse so as to make his action the more magnificent and striking, you must refrain from pulling at his mouth with the bit as well as from spurring and whipping him. But if you teach your horse to go with a light hand on the bit, and yet to hold his head well up and to arch his neck, you will be making him do just what the animal himself glories and delights in*"

Xenophon, *The Art of Horsemanship*

Xenophon, a Greek riding master, wrote the *The Art of Horsemanship*. Xenophon holds the distinction of writing the very first (but not last) completely surviving dressage book. This is a good book, and Xenophon was a good guy. His teachings were considered quite radical at the time. He believed, you see, that horses should be treated humanely. This was truly a revolutionary concept. However, lest we pass judgment, when's the last time you hugged your car? Xenophon was also was the first to lay on the guilt trip about pulling back on the reins. That's one way to tell the good guys from the bad guys!

Remarkably, copies of Xenophon's *The Art of Horsemanship* are available today at your favorite online booksellers. Think about this: For instance, Attila the Hun, another noted equestrian, had the Roman Empire on the run in 450 A.D., some 900 years *after* Xenophon's time! Needless to say, Xenophon's work has shown some kind of staying power.

Federico Grisone (Sometime in the 1500s)

After what was an incredibly long dry spell for the publication of dressage books, along came Federico Grisone. On or about 1550, Federico Grisone, an Italian riding master, wrote the second (but not last) dressage book, the title roughly translated to *Riding Rules*. This book was an international bestseller at the time. This was not especially good news for horses trained in dressage. Grisone, you see, interpreted the works of Xenophon. However, he missed the part about being kind to horses in his translation.

The methods outlined in Grisone's book were used to train war horses and stressed complete obedience. For example, Grisone often recommended beating the recalcitrant horse over the head. In fairness, you know there have been times you've felt the same way. And here's a good one, if your horse won't go forward, take a bundle of straw, light it on fire and hold in under his tail! This was very effective, but it does require a skilled and nimble assistant working on the ground. Whips and spurs played a big role in his training methods. However, he did discuss good stuff like gymnastic training; he was on the right track in that.

Forward, I say!

One of Grisone's most noted students, Pignatelli, was a big bit guy. He developed a bit that bears his name—the Pignatelli Bit. Pignatelli's bit was pretty nasty but widely used through the 18th Century. Pictures of Pignatelli's bit will leave you gasping in horror. Pignatelli, like Grisone, was considered quite the horseman in his time.

Antoine de Pluvinel (1556–1620)

> **"**We shall take care not to vex the horse, or cause it to abandon its affable gracefulness in disgust. For this is like the fragrance blossoms, which never again returns once it has vanished.**"**
>
> **Antoine de Pluvinel, Le Manage Royal**

Thank heavens for Pluvinel! On or about 1620, Pluvinel's book *Le Manage Royal* was published posthumously. Pluvinel, a French riding master, was a student of the bit guy, Pignatelli. Despite this, Pluvinel must have dusted off a copy of Xenophon's old book and actually got the part about being nice to the horse.

Pluvinel rejected the heavy spurring and extremely harsh bits, and believed beatings should be used sparingly. He was credited with inventing training in "pillars," which is both good and bad. Evidently, training in pillars, something not practiced by Intro and Training Level riders, can be pretty harsh in the wrong hands. It has something to do with tying a horse between two posts and holding burning straw under his tail to achieve piaffe—if you happen to be reading Grisone's bestseller, that is!

Pluvinel also introduced the "carousels" to music, which we know today as quadrilles. He was the Reiner Klimke of his day, marveled and revered for his exquisite form on horseback. Being one of the good guys, he stressed the importance of making riders feel guilty about pulling back on the reins. However, in contrast to other great masters, his admonishments were gracefully stated in poetic language. "The fragrance blossoms that will *never* again return," he warns. Isn't that lovely? That refrain is certainly under-utilized by today's trainers of Intro and Training Level riders, who are haplessly jerking back on the horse's mouth and ruining the "fragrance blossoms" forever.

William Cavendish, Duke of Newcastle (1592–1676)

The Duke wrote two dressage books. In 1658, there was *General System of Horsemanship* followed by *The New Way to Break in Horses*. The Duke is somewhat controversial. Some hail his methods as humane, while others deride his harsh methods of collection. He is credited with the invention of draw reins. He was also very much into complete obedience of the horse and his own self-worship, according to some less-than-keen reviewers. Most would agree the man had a big ego. He was a Duke, after all.

On a more positive note, the copperplate illustrations in his books were unanimously considered great. Also, a small piece of trivia: his second wife, Margaret, 30 years his junior (a trophy wife?), was one of the world's earliest feminists. The Duke was evidently cool with that. Perhaps he saved his autocratic control-freak tendencies for his horses? And lastly, the Duke simply adored Spanish horses. He is widely quoted as proclaiming them the most beautiful creatures on earth.

François Robichon de la Guérinière (1688–1751)

"Suppleness and lack of restraint are the prerequisites for voluntarily offered obedience, not for agonized subjection of the horse."

François Robichon de la Guérinière

This Frenchman's book, *L'Ecole de Cavalerie* was published in 1733. This one is easy. De la Guérinière was a great guy! First and foremost, he advocated the complete end to torturing horses. His training methods emphasized a partnership with the horse with *no* beatings. In addition, he limited the use of pillars and generally revolutionized the art of dressage.

The mere mention of de la Guérinière's name causes the best of the classical, accomplished horsemen worldwide to sigh mistily and surreptitiously wipe away tears. Dressage horses correctly trained in de la Guérinière's methods are similarly affected. Thank you, dear François!

On the downside for aspiring Intro and Training Level riders, de la Guérinière is credited with the invention of the half halt and the shoulder-in. This no doubt was an elitist thing to keep out the riffraff. The Spanish Riding School of Vienna is still heavily influenced by de la Guérinière's teachings. Definitely a great guy, except for the half halt and shoulder-in!

François Baucher (1796–1873)

> **"**Many an old trainer is honest enough to admit that he did not become a sensible and fine rider until he lost most of his physical strength and that, since then, he obtains from his horse in a calm and reliable manner everything which in the past he had thought could be accomplished only after a hard struggle.**"**
> **Gustav Steinbrecht, The Gymnasium of the Horse**

Baucher is yet another French riding master and one-time circus performer. Baucher's book *Methods of the Art of Riding According to New Principles* was published in 1843. Baucher's methods were controversial, so it's difficult for the average Intro and Training Level rider to conclude if he was a great guy or a really bad guy.

Baucher was all about collection. He was also a "get it done quick" sort of fellow. Unlike other great masters, Baucher was not royally born and had to actually work for a living. This could explain his more pragmatic get-it-done attitude. Baucher really had two distinct phases to his career: In the early years he was rumored to be quite harsh in his methods, including forced muzzling and other mean stuff.

Fortunately, in the midst of his colorful career, the story goes that Baucher was struck down in a riding hall by a great chandelier. Angered horse god, perhaps? Although he recovered from his extensive injuries, he remained quite weakened physically. In his more delicate state, he became renowned for some of his most brilliant riding and much gentler methods of horsemanship.

His teaching influenced the famous French riding school, the Cadre Noir in Saumur. Baucher is credited with inventing the one-tempi changes at the canter. Even more impressive though, Baucher performed the backward canter. A *backward* canter! While perhaps dismissed as a mere circus trick by accomplished riders, the idea of cantering *backwards* is astounding to those of us struggling to get the correct, left lead, *forward* canter.

Gustav Steinbrecht (1808–1885)

"The skill of the hands can justifiably be considered a measure of the rider's total skill. ... A person who really has bad hands can never be a rider in the true sense of the word, no matter how firm his seat, how much courage and elegance of appearance he displays. His fault is the product of a lack of feel for, and understanding of, the horse."

Gustav Steinbrecht, The Gymnasium of the Horse

In 1885 came Gustav Steinbrecht's oft-mentioned *The Gymnasium of the Horse*. A German veterinarian and riding master, Steinbrecht was heavily influenced by de la Guérinière's work and was basically opposed to Baucher's methods—you know how these guys love to fight! In Steinbrecht's book the golden rule is, "Ride your horse forward and set it straight." Sound familiar? Of course to ride your horse forward and straighten him requires a great deal of 20-meter circles as well as all those baffling lateral movements. Go figure. Or rather—go do school figures.

Steinbrecht generously details all the required circles and school figures necessary to straighten your horse. He also spends a great deal of time making you feel guilty about pulling back on the reins. Steinbrecht is therefore one of the good guys.

Gymnasium, which was published posthumously, is considered the "bible" of the German School of riding. Remarkably, the English translation of the German 10th Edition of *Gymnasium* was published by Xenophon Press. That's right—Xenophon—as in our very first Greek master. Truly, dressage is all about circles, in some cosmic sense.

In Summary

So there you have it—the *Cliffs Notes* to great dressage books by the great dressage guys. Here is one important note in this history lesson: The evolution of the art of dressage also involved the evolution of the type of horse used. From Xenophon's time until around the 1600s the horse of choice was the Spanish or Iberian horse, a horse naturally gifted in collection. As the military styles changed, a more warmblood-type horse emerged. The Spanish horse would remain, for the most part, limited to secret horse societies like the Spanish Riding School. De la Guérinière and Steinbrecht's teachings were aimed at this warmblood-style horse.

So in essence, there are two styles of dressage. One is the *haute école*—performed as an end in itself and utilizing Iberian horses. The other is military dressage, a more pragmatic sport that uses the warmblood-type horse. These two types of horses require different training methods to develop upper-level dressage movements. Hence, the ongoing battles between the Classical (Iberian) School and the Competitive (warmblood) School.

To further confuse the issue, there are the classicalists within the Competitive School and, to a lesser degree; there are competitive riders within the Classical School. This certainly muddies the waters when it comes to classifying who's who and deciding which side to take.

Regardless, the training of horses in dressage throughout the centuries has certainly included the development of some pretty interesting gadgets for use in developing harmony with the horse. Some of these gadgets remain popular today and are used even by Intro and Training Level riders who don't actually do any dressage. So here is how the "tools of the trade" will work for you:

The Perfect Dressage Saddle

Ha, ha! I know you're laughing at this one! You don't need a book for this. There is *no* such thing as the perfect dressage saddle. Even the very greenest of dressage riders are painfully aware of this terrible fact. That will not, however, prevent you from spending thousands upon thousands of dollars seeking the perfect dressage saddle. This is an essential requirement of dressage.

This horrid fact can be blamed on de la Guérinière. That's right, he actually cared how saddle fit affected the movement of the horse. He was the genius who designed the "new" dressage saddle. Prior to that, all the other guys used something known as the "forked seat" saddle. Apparently, the leg aids were not effective in the old style saddle, hence de la Guérinière's invention. This fact, along with half halt and shoulder-in, makes you wonder about this de la Guérinière dude. Did he have it in for Intro and Training Level riders, or what?

The problem with dressage saddles is they are meant to help the horse achieve On the Bit. Therefore, it must fit the horse's back perfectly without impeding the development of his back muscles. Intro and Training Level riders never develop any back muscles in their horse, but you're still required to try. Furthermore, this magical saddle must fit the *rider* perfectly as well. Only with the perfect saddle will the rider achieve the perfect seat, which leads to achieving the perfect version of On the Bit.

You will be excited when you buy your first (but not last) dressage saddle. Your investment symbolizes your commitment to the art. However, you will sell your first (but not last) dressage saddle about the same time you sell your first (but not last) dressage horse, because it won't fit your second (but not last) dressage horse. You will most likely have to move to a more expensive model in both horse and saddle. This vicious cycle will continue unabated throughout your dressage journey.

The Dressage Whip

Here is an instrument you will be handed immediately at the beginnings of your dressage journey: the dressage whip. Yes, even Intro and Training Level riders may use this tool. Previously you used the whip for those unfortunate occasions when your horse refused to cross a stream or ran out from a jump. Not anymore! You will be admonished immediately and sternly that the dressage whip is used as an *aid*, not as an instrument of punishment.

One of first problems encountered with the dressage whip is its length. It is longer than the "crop" you were used to. You simply cannot help accidentally smacking your horse with this long, awkward whip. This usually occurs at the worst possible moment, like when you're asking for the downward transition from the canter, and your horse ends up bolting across the arena because you are inadvertently smacking him with the whip. Oops! You will spend a lot of time apologizing profusely to your horse until you become adept at handling your dressage whip.

Another skill to develop is the switching of your whip so it is always carried on the inside. Given that in dressage we perform countless circles and many changes of directions, clearly this is an issue. Here you will end up smacking yourself in the face and dropping the reins and ruining your lovely trot across the diagonal and so forth. It's quite embarrassing. At any rate, it takes quite a few years to master the use of the dressage whip, which in theory is supposed to be a delicate complement to your leg aids.

Strangely enough, the use of the dressage whip is absolutely essential in training, but is not allowed while performing in championship competitions. That rule is rather cruel—to the rider that is—since it's hard to get your horse to go suitably forward while pulling him into the On the Bit position at the same time. Yet another great mystery surrounding dressage competitions and one of the reasons some folks switch to the Other School, which, if you recall, is still boycotting competitions.

Spurs

> **"**A 'jab with the spurs' is the strongest and most emphatic influence with the spurs. It gives the horse a momentary, intense pain and, by injuring the skin, causes infection and swelling of the parts involved so that, for some time, the sensitivity at that point is even greater. I speak of course of spurs that really deserve their name and are equipped with five-to-six point rowels. ... Lazy horses and those that are reluctant to use their power are driven into lively action by a jab with the spur; and any stubbornness, resistance, or mischievousness is punished with the spurs. ...A 'prick with the spurs' is no punishment but an aid.**"**
> **Gustav Steinbrecht, The Gymnasium of the Horse**

Have you ever heard the expression "earning your spurs"? Thankfully, we don't have to earn them in dressage. Even Intro and Training Level riders may strap on a set of spurs from the onset of their training. It doesn't matter if your seat isn't fully, or even minutely, developed. Spurs are absolutely mandatory in dressage. As explained in the Chapter 5: Origins of Dressage, spurs have been a time-honored instrument used by the greatest of the great, and the worst of the worst. Some things never change.

Like the dressage whip, the spur is regarded as an extension (as opposed to lengthening) of your aids. It is used delicately to reinforce your leg. How does this translate for the Intro and Training Level rider? The use of the spur is encouraged because your first, second, third (but not last) trainer simply cannot stand to see you kicking away pathetically to get your horse going forward. This method "dulls" your horse to the leg aids.

Therefore, strap on spurs, give a quick jab or two, and off your horse goes. It is really much more humane than using Grisone's method of achieving forward—holding burning straw beneath the horse's tail. This way your trainer can concentrate on you, rather than leaping out of the way of a bolting horse.

The length of your spur will increase the longer you ride. You see, after a while, your horse will become immune to the jabbing of your little spur. Hence, you move up a size. This process continues right up to the Grand Prix levels. Grand Prix riders are rumored to have a great deal of difficulty walking in their spurs because of their enormous size. And while dressage whips are banned from championship competitions, spurs are actually required pieces of equipment at the highest FEI levels.

It should be noted that on some occasions, dressage horses actually have spur marks on their sides. Blood has even been drawn. This is frowned upon by both the Classical and the Competitive Schools of dressage. This is one area where they are in agreement because there have been culprits from both schools guilty of spurring too vigorously.

The On the Bit Bit

> **"**However, the fact of the matter is that a double bridle gives the rider more control over the horse. This is true whether the rider is a master or relative novice to the equipment. The control can be used skillfully to obtain, for example, more elevation and cadence in the trot, or it can be used to keep the horse's head down—and everything in between.**"**
>
> **MsKreuz "Double Bridle in Third Level???" 10/13/02, UDBB**

The ultimate On the Bit bit is the double bridle. Double bridle is really a misnomer here, because what we are talking about is the use of double bits. That's right—the horse is ridden with both a snaffle bit *and* a curb bit in his mouth. Some things haven't changed since the time of Frederico Grisone and Pignatelli, "The Bit Guy."

As Intro and Training Level riders are not allowed to use double bridles, this is merely a theoretical discussion. A great deal of skill is required to correctly manipulate the two bits, each of which comes with its own set of reins. The rider must use either the snaffle rein or the curb rein depending upon the movement. One does have to ponder how all that stuff actually fits into the horse's mouth. You'd think the horse would run screaming in the opposite direction when he sees that rig coming his way. Sometimes one simply has to take a moment to admire equine stoicism.

The use of the double bridle is not accepted in the dressage arena until Third Level. It used to be Fourth Level until yet another battle was lost by the Classical School to the Competitive School. Really, the Classical School is a bit like the ineffectual, yet annoying, Green Party in the United States. You know how the Green Party never misses an opportunity to make us feel bad about things like holes in the ozone layer and global warming? Likewise bent on making everyone feel guilty, the Classical School spends a great deal of time wagging their fingers at the position of the curb bit. They seem to feel it is excessively engaged.

Intro and Training Level riders will most likely never use a double bridle. They are condemned to a lifetime of searching for a single bit that will produce the magical effects of the double bridle. The masters did graciously design some helpful tools for the single bit rider, mostly in the form of various types of nosebands.

For some unknown reason, it is helpful to tie the horse's mouth closed with such contraptions as the Crank and the drop noseband. Apparently this may assist in the all-important softening of the jaw, although the logic escapes most Intro and Training riders. The important thing to remember about the various nosebands is to tighten them as much as possible before your lessons. While riding on your own, you may loosen them, much to the relief of you and your horse.

Draw Reins

"*In the wrong hands, draw reins are as dangerous as razorblades in the hand of a monkey***"**
Col. Alois Podhajsky, Director, Spanish Riding School of Vienna

Draw reins, ah! As pointed out in Chapter 5: Origins of Dressage, draw reins were invented, or at least popularized, by the Duke of Newcastle. They are a hideous, yet glorious invention indeed! Since Intro and Training Level riders cannot use the double bridle, draw reins are your ultimate On the Bit tool.

Really, if you don't look at it too closely, draw reins are a marvelous thing. Basically, they are pair of lunge-line type reins. They are threaded through the horse's bit and secured between his front legs at the girth or on the side, below each saddle flap. They are held in your hands, so you are essentially dealing with two sets of reins. Once you've mastered this cumbersome arrangement, you will be full of pride; this is just like the double bridle!

You will about expire from delight the first few times you ride in draw reins. Previously, your attempts at On the Bit had very inconsistent results. Your horse would fling his head up, then down, then side to side—anywhere but the On the Bit position. Not anymore! That head goes up—bang! Pull back on both sets of reins and by golly your horse brings his head down instantly! Why? Draw reins work on the principle of leverage. Because the draw reins are attached to an immovable piece of equipment—the girth—you have far greater power over the horse's head and neck. When you pull back on the reins, you essentially catch the horse's head and neck between the hand and the girth! There ain't no escape! Ha, ha! No more giraffe neck!

What is so terrible about this, you might wonder? Well, some argue there is nothing particularly wrong with this arrangement. However, it is fraught with dangers to the Intro and Training Level riders, who, in the first place, forget to ever release the pressure on draw reins. That hurts. Remember, Intro and Training Level riders are obsessed with On the Bit, not with dressage (although you don't realize it). This On the Bit position created by the draw reins is artificial because the horse is not using his back and, generally, his head is forced too low. In real dressage, the goal is to have the horse pushing from behind, supple in his back, with his head up and open.

The gaits of the horse are usually not improved by being forced to tool about in this cramped position. They will perform the "draw rein shuffle" to compensate for having their head drawn to their chest. That is similar to the gait you use when crossing a slippery sidewalk after a snowstorm—head down and mincing steps.

In addition, the moment the draw reins are removed, your poor horse is even more resistant to getting the On the Bit position. Horses generally exhibit one of two unmistakable signs of draw rein riding: The first is the "curled up" defeatist posture—his way of cry-ing "uncle!" Or your horse will carry his head and neck in the angry, giraffe posture, clearly refusing to submit voluntarily. Either way, your task of achieving On the Bit is now harder than ever.

This is why you will enjoy this invention for only a limited time. Eventually it will be pointed out to you, in no uncertain terms, that you have no business using draw reins on your poor horse. Perhaps a highly skilled rider who knows how to actually release the pressure on the horse's mouth, can use draw reins effectively. But rest assured, you do not qualify. You do not have the necessary independent seat and hands, timing and finesse to make this anything less than an instrument of torture to your horse. Razor blades in the hands of monkeys, indeed!

Heartbroken, you give up your draw reins. This is a one of few moments in your dressage career that you will feel good, because you've done the "right thing." You've chosen to pursue the ideal. You go back to yanking, pulling and kicking because you are committed to being a good dressage rider. But you will never throw your draw reins away. They will remain, fondly, secretly tucked away—like a picture of your old boyfriend—at the bottom of your ever-growing tack trunk.

Side Reins

> **"**No discussion of work on the lunge, which is so often minimized, neglected, or misused, should fail to point out an error made more and more often in recent years. Instead of the lunge rein being clasped to the cavesson, it is fastened to the ring of the snaffle, which is not only incorrect but also absolutely harmful. Lungeing like this is nonsense and brutality, placing laziness and desire for quick work above consideration for the animal.**"**
> **Col. Alois Podhajsky, My Horses, My Teachers**

Side reins are another piece of dressage equipment you will quickly become familiar with. Unlike draw reins, side reins are good. They are two lengths of leather or webbing that attach from the girth below the saddle flaps to the bit on each side. Of course, more correctly, they should attach to a cavesson and surcingle, which are pieces of equipment you will avoid purchasing until you are truly at the edge. Side reins are used when you are lungeing your horse. They act as the reins and, when fitted incorrectly, will instantly have the horse On the Bit.

There are two things here that need to be explained: Your use of side reins will be essentially meaningless in training your horse, because you don't know how to fit them properly or how to lunge the horse correctly. But they're not generally harmful, so it is a skill you can enjoy practicing to enhance your battered self-esteem.

That is until the second thing is explained. That's right—you've probably guessed it—lungeing in side reins can be a bad thing. Great controversy abounds over the correct adjustment of side reins. Too tight, which puts the horse On the Bit, is vigorously opposed by some. It is suggested that a green horse (yours) should be lunged in loose side reins, thereby seeking On the Bit on his own. This is because you will be encouraging the engagement of the hindquarters, hence lungeing back to front. You will find this just as difficult to achieve while lungeing as it is when riding. You will almost inevitably shorten the side reins to achieve On the Bit, but you will feel bad about it. Eventually, you will just give up lungeing entirely.

The truly desperate will also try riding in side reins. In this case, the side reins will be attached loosely, because otherwise you risk killing yourself and your horse if he should object to this confinement. It's a no brainer. You will do this in hopes of achieving On the Bit. It will not work. But at least no one will question your determination to achieve On the Bit.

My Mostly Pathetic Attempts at Using the Tools of the Trade

I tried several "tools of the trade" in my search for On the Bit. I used draw reins with my first (but not last) dressage horse, Chad. Granted, they were handed to me my first (but not last) trainer, so I can honestly proclaim my ignorance to the High Court of Classicalists from both schools. To this day, I have a picture of Chad hanging on my dressage wall of fame/shame. I was so proud of that picture. There we were, trotting down the long side of the arena, and Chad was On the Bit! Of course, I was riding him in draw reins. Now that I'm farther along in my journey, I cringe at the picture. Sure, we were On the Bit, but we were also performing the "draw rein shuffle."

I've been very resistant to using the dressage whip. Honestly, I'm just not that coordinated. While I have used the whip at various times with all my dressage horses, I've always hated it. I have a hard enough time trying to control the reins without dealing with a whip. I generally end up smacking myself in the face with it. That should tell you something about my hands!

I also hate using spurs. Why? Because, being the opposite of a Dressage Queen, I generally ride in a pair of bargain-basement, ill-fitting half chaps. Attempting to strap on a pair of spurs over these stretched-out pieces of suede is not only time consuming but they never fit correctly. You can at least rest assured that my one pair of hardly used spurs are those itty-bitty baby spurs, the kind that real dressage riders laugh at.

Truly the funniest, or perhaps most pathetic, thing I ever did was ride Gus, my second (but not last) dressage horse, in side reins. I'd given up my draw reins and now belonged to the correct, classical, purist school of yank and kick. During this period I perfected my lungeing skills. OK, well not really. As I mentioned earlier, I'm not the most coordinated individual. I think I've had moments worthy of America's Funniest Home Videos just in my attempts to gather up the lunge line before I even began lungeing! That dang thing had to be 500 feet long! I've tripped over and been tangled by the lunge line more times than I care to remember. Then again, it wouldn't be pointed out to me until the TFO era, that one needs to stand fairly still while lungeing. Poor Gus, we'd run haphazardly about the entire ring, performing endless potato-shaped circles. Gus was ever the good sport.

Finally, I came upon the brilliant idea to actually ride in side reins. Did I mention that Gus was a wonderful soul? He actually put up with all my wacky ideas without ever harming a hair on my head. And at the time, he was only 5 years old! Saint Gus! My riding in side reins didn't last very long. For one thing, it did not help us achieve On the Bit. But even more so, I just got disgusted with the amount of time it took to get him tacked up to ride. You know how the old saying goes: You can take the girl out of the hack stable, but you can't take the hack stable out of the girl.

You might be curious about whatever happened to my first and second (but not last) dressage horses, Chad and Gus. Well, ironically enough, they both live with my second (but not last) trainer, Gail. I will be forever fond of Gail. She tried harder than any trainer before or since to teach me On the Bit. I can only imagine the suffering I put her through! As you can appreciate, attempting to teach me On the Bit is a thankless task.

Gail also has a great appreciation for my taste in horses. Chad belongs to one of her adult students, who, fortunately, already has a big dressage horse. Chad is her "fun" horse. You know, when she's ready to weep from frustration with her "big" horse, she jumps on Chad and goes on a trail ride. Gus is owned by one of Gail's teenage students. Yes, a lovely young woman with legs a mile long and natural talent. Much to my chagrin, she easily achieves On the Bit with Gus, and together they've gone on to win several championships in dressage and eventing on the local circuit. Yes, my Saint Gus is a hotshot now and I believe fully recovered from the trauma of having been ridden in side reins.

I believe Gail is actually planning on building a wing on her barn to accommodate all my failed dressage prospects. I sometimes wonder if she's gleefully rubbing her hands together in anticipation of getting my magnificent "Gray Ponies," TFO and Chico, when I hit yet another brick wall on my dressage journey. ■

CHAPTER SIX
Walking the Dark Side
(The Misadventures of Poor Boo-Boo Head)

By now, one can only hope you have a clear picture of how very muddled the path of dressage can be. Some important themes just cannot be stressed enough. Like, one should never pull back on the reins of your dressage horse, but you do it anyway. And no matter what tools of the trade you use, you will be using them incorrectly. There is only one correct way to correctly learn correct dressage, and your way is not the correct way.

Believe or not, it gets worse! That's right. I think you know what I'm talking about. You've scanned through this chapter with a sinking feeling in your stomach. First, you were hoping to find some really cool pictures. It's understandable. After all, you just finished the scholarly, eyes-crossing chapter on the "origins of dressage" and the "tools of the trade." But here, you suspect someone may have been spying on some of your schooling sessions with your first, second or third (but not last) dressage horse. Or perhaps someone has rifled through your secret file of horse bookkeeping paperwork. Could it be?

Yes, let us now take a walk on the dark side. First, let's talk about the mind boggling amount of money you are spending on your journey. And then let's turn to those very ugly emotions you've experienced—fear, frustration and rage—while seeking to dance with your horse. Shall we?

The Cost of Dressage

> **"**My husband does not understand why I do not know how to ride yet. I have been taking consistent dressage lessons for about three years. He tells me that if I can't figure out how to make my horse stop, go and turn by now that I may want to consider taking up another sport! He has come to watch a couple of my shows and is very happy when I win, but he is not a horseperson at all and does not understand everything that goes into it (time, money and lots of work). I get comments like, "I could own a Ferrari for what we spend on that horse.**"**
> **Gracie Lou, "How non-horsey husband sees it," 7/3/03, UDBB**

It is distressing to speak of something as crass as money when we are engaged in pursuing an art form. But when you are spending upward of $1,000 per year just on dressage books, you realize your obsession is beginning to take a serious toll on your checkbook. For those who shy away from tracking costs, think about your dressage library. You buy about 15 dressage books a year. The average cost is $24.99. Add on $6 each for shipping and handling from amazon.com. That's $464.85 and that doesn't include the must-have collector's edition of De la Guérinière's classic, for which you paid $425 plus $25 shipping, handling and insurance. So, in one year you've spent $914.85 on books, and all you've done is read the fore-word and prologue and looked at some cool pictures. Let's not even delve into what you pay for your dressage videos! This is not sane.

It wasn't always this bad. When you first started dressage, your expenses were on the par with anyone who kept a horse, and grant-ed horses are not a cheap hobby. However, there is a big difference between dabbling in a hobby and pursuing art, particularly an art as elusive as dressage. Initially you expected to take lessons once a week. Yes, they were expensive, but you figured it was manageable. You only needed to take them long enough to achieve On the Bit. Once a week lessons: Ha, ha! That didn't last long.

Now you are paying your trainer to school your horse several times a week in a desperate effort to teach him On the Bit, so you don't have to sell him. You know from the study of the foreword in your dressage books, that dressage involves gymnastic training of the horse. Riding once or twice a week just doesn't cut it. Since you are now working triple overtime to pay off you horse expenses, you don't have time to do more than take two lessons during the week. On the weekends you are taking expensive clinics with big name trainers. The only way to keep your horse in shape is to pay a pro-fessional to ride him while you're at work. So basically, your lesson and training fees are running more than five figures per year.

And, of course, that's not all. You now understand the importance of having your horse in peak condition. Everyone knows, after all, the reason why most horses can't achieve On the Bit is because they are suffering from some physical distress. This requires bi-monthly visits from both the horse chiropractor and the equine massage therapist. Your farrier is a dressage horse specialist and the most expensive guy in the county. He does your horse's feet every four weeks. Your equine dentist visits your horse more often than you visit your dentist. And, we mustn't forget to mention the monthly visits from the state-of-the-art vet to administer various hock injections and the like.

Eventually, as you become more sophisticated, you will spend a lot of time online exploring various herbal supplements that enhance your horse's ability to achieve On the Bit. You will indulge in the entire holistic approach, in addition to all the above-mentioned traditional practices despite the fact they are inherently contradictory methods.

You will find it necessary, after a while, to consult with an animal communicator on a regular basis, to discuss your horse's angst-filled emotions regarding On the Bit. This is most helpful. Animal communicators are much like hairdressers. They spend as much time psychoanalyzing you as they do asking your horse if he likes his corner stall. This is some of the best money you've spent. Heaven knows, you need a little stroking at this point.

And, of course, you have placed on retainer the services of a master saddle fitter. This is because every time you consult with one of the other professionals you have on staff, they suggest that your horse is uncomfortable because of saddle fit. You will have your saddle reflocked (you know what this is now) and adjusted several times before giving up and buying a new one.

So obviously, maintaining your dressage skills and keeping your dressage horse in peak condition, all in order to achieve On the Bit, does not happen with merely once-a-week lessons. It requires a formidable staff of professionals working around the clock. This, of course, comes with a hefty price tag.

Dealing with the Cost of Dressage

Early on, you will learn various strategies for coping with all this necessary expense. First you will dedicate a single credit card for all your online purchases. Once the balance owed on your credit card soars over four figures, you will get a post office box. This way, you can receive your monthly bill without risk of exposure to your spouse or significant other. He will see your credit card bill only once, and you'll appreciate the importance of this strategy. You will also become adept at surfing credit cards to keep the interest payments under four figures a year.

In addition, you will set up a separate checking account for your horse-keeping expenses. Again, this is to protect your loved one from unnecessary distress. He really doesn't need to worry his pretty little head about this. The monthly statement will be directed to your secret P.O. Box as an added precaution.

After a while, you will stop sharing the news about your new saddle purchases. He doesn't need to know, and saddles all look the same to him anyway. In fact, after a while, he'll never have to know when you've purchased yet another dressage horse. He can't be expected to understand the urgency of getting a schoolmaster trained to

Fourth Level. Just try to stay with the same color horses and use endearing nicknames, like Boo-Boo Head, when referring to them.

Your spouse or significant other will be very impressed the one or two times a year he sees you ride. He will marvel at how well you are achieving On the Bit. He thinks you still own that little Quarter Horse when, in fact, you are mounted on your Dutch Warmblood imported from Europe. This is your way of showing you care. It's quite heartwarming.

Another benefit derived from your expenditures is satisfaction in the knowledge that you are doing your part to drive the sometimes floundering economy. Despite a recession here or there, your spending has continued unabated. It makes you proud to do your part as an American.

And in a global economy, the fact that many of your dollars go to Germany to buy horses, and England for tack is another source of satisfaction. No, you've turned your back on countries like China and Taiwan who have sucked the manufacturing business right out of the United States. Instead, the bulk of your support goes to the European Union. Indeed, it is rumored that dressage riders have been responsible for salvaging the sometimes-strained relationship between Germany and the United States. Truly, you are on the cutting edge of the new global economy and world peace.

So, despite your enormous expenditures on behalf of your dressage journey, it really isn't all that bad. Your horse is living in the lap of luxury, his every need catered to. Your relationship skills have been finely honed. Your spouse or significant other was delighted when you actually encouraged him to take up golfing so you'd have some leverage when he started yelling about the time and money spent on your journey. And finally, you are a fine, upstanding member of the global community who helps maintain good relations with other countries. Really it's not all so bad.

Of course, there is the triple overtime you are forced to work to keep abreast of your spending. But even so, there is an upside. You are no doubt sitting in front of a computer all day, so you can combine work and pleasure by visiting your online dressage sites while at work. Indeed, your true mastery is not of dressage—of course. No, you have achieved a really remarkable, productive and wholesome balance of home, avocation and work. This is truly cutting edge stuff!

Fear

Having successfully dealt with the costs of dressage, we are left with some of the uglier issues associated with our journey. Early on in *Survival Guide*, we discussed the widely held view that dressage riders are wimps. It was suggested that this reputation was somewhat unfair. Dressage riders are truly intellectuals in pursuit of the noble goal of achieving the perfect 20-meter circle while On the Bit. This is true. However, it is only part of the equation.

The role of fear and its influence on our horsemanship is rarely discussed, at least with any straightforward honesty. But let's face the facts: As middle class, middle-aged white women our tolerance for the more exuberant equine behavior diminishes in a predictable fashion once we pass the age of 30. It is pretty basic human survival instinct and nothing to be ashamed of. Quite simply, as we get older, we don't rebound quite as easily from "kissing the dirt." Not as easily at all. It hurts! Our backs, our knees, our necks—and our psyches —all lose elasticity with age.

Getting Launched

> **"**Thank goodness I was wearing my helmet because I had this lovely canter going and the next thing I was flying through the air. Landed on my fanny and then hit my head hard. Still dealing with a headache from hell. My mare has been a bit lively here lately, which is nice to ride if I can channel it, but today she exploded before I even knew what was coming.**"**
>
> Galliegirl "My mare launched me today," 1/5/04, *UDBB*

Think back to the tumbles you took as a kid, being bucked off by some enthusiastic young horse. Remember how you dusted yourself off, chagrined, and remounted the crazy bronc with an utter lack of fear. The thing that stung the worst was your pride. You probably weren't even wearing a helmet!

Picture that same tumble when you're 40 years old. Imagine you are engrossed in a typical school routine. Perhaps you are perfecting your walk-to-canter transitions. As you ask your horse to lift up elegantly into a canter with that delicate timing of crank, spur and whip—he suddenly bolts out from underneath you. You clamp your legs and pull back hard, but he merely yanks the reins out of your hands and begins to buck explosively across the arena. You're not sure what went wrong, but it doesn't matter. By the second perfectly executed buck you are launched airborne from the saddle and land in a twisted heap on the arena floor, stunned by the ferocity of the fall.

You may or may not rise from the dust. If you do, it will be slowly. Very, very slowly. Your legs will be quivering and your hands shaking as reaction sets in. Best case scenario, you will, at a snail's pace, brush the dirt from your once-pristine riding breeches. You will check for bruises and breaks, and arch your back gingerly. Finally and carefully, you move your head back and forth, testing for whiplash.

At this point, your horse is calmly munching grass at the other end of the arena with one ear cast warily in your direction. Understanding what must be done, you ever so painstakingly catch your errant mount and lead him back to the mounting block. And you remount, hoping against hope there will be no more bucking episodes. Once mounted, you hold the reins in a death grip and ask your horse to walk around the arena—once. Then you put the horse away, go home and call your chiropractor.

That is the best case scenario. There can be much more serious consequences to getting launched. Who among us has not suppressed a shudder or perhaps even shed a tear over the fate of the late actor Christopher Reeves? Ironically best known for his starring role in the motion picture *Superman*, this handsome and charismatic movie star became permanently disabled as the result of an eventing accident. And while, to date, there have been no high profile fatalities suffered at dressage competitions, we have all been privy to tragic stories of equine-related deaths. Given these possible consequences, the fear of getting launched is not necessarily an irrational emotion.

Getting Launched

The Effects of Fear

"*Fear stinks. Having been through the ugly fall thing myself enough in my life, and having dealt with so many students who were completely terrified of their horses, I've seen how hard it is just to get on. I think it's harder, too, the older you get. I know I always have this picture in my mind of me being so old and brittle now, that if I hit the ground I will break into a million little pieces. At least, that's how my body feels!*"

Webasaur, "Repairing trust," 1/13/04, UDBB

So it is simple: As we age, our tolerance for extreme sports diminishes. While dressage in itself may not qualify as an extreme sport, any endeavor involving horses has inherent dangers. Despite the innate generosity of these creatures, they are still prisoners of their own genetics. They are large and powerful and wired for "flight or fight."

But human nature is a complex beast. We have a difficult time reconciling what is in our heart and mind with the demands and ability of our bodies. So we deny reality and rationalize our fearful behavior. Not to keep picking on Germany, but remember, for example, Hitler convinced a nation of ordinary, hardworking and civilized people to turn a blind eye to genocide. Likewise, the people of the United States condoned the decimation of the Native Americans and the enslavement of Africans. And these are but a few cases in point of what the human mind is capable of rationalizing. Never underestimate this powerful and uniquely human behavior. Our ability to rationalize our fear and project the blame outward can be breathtaking in scope. Really, denying our fear of getting hurt by our horse is child's play for the human mind.

There are several very important ramifications to fear and dressage. First and foremost, with careful study of the books, which you have done, you will come to understand—intellectually—that dressage is about "letting go." In order to achieve that miraculous connection— that perfect seat, those light hands—you must let go mentally and physically. One of the earliest bestsellers, a precursor to the dressage books, is Sally Swift's *Centered Riding*. In it you will read exhortations of allowing your legs to "drape your horse like wet noodles." This will be very difficult to do, because of fear, when your legs are a vise grip, not a wet noodle.

Furthermore, horses are incredibly sensitive creatures. They can smell your fear a mile away, before you even get out of the car and walk to the barn. Your fear makes them very, very nervous. They figure you must know something they don't. So if you're afraid, they're afraid. Until you conquer your fear, expect your next rides to be very nerve-wracking for both you and your horse.

To make matters worse, you are no doubt at a barn with other dressage riders. These middle-aged ladies are fearful, too. You discuss your mutual spills in gruesome detail. You relive each and every moment of your last fall and dissect all the possible causes of your horse's bucking episode. You are sure your horse is to blame. Before long, as you look at Boo-Boo Head standing casually in his stall, he takes on sinister proportions in your mind.

It works like this. As you get the increasingly jumpy Boo-Boo Head ready to ride, your dressage friends ask if you want the EMT to be on standby. They suggest you should lunge Boo-Boo Head for a good half hour before attempting to swing a leg over. Perhaps a half cc of ace would be in order? By the time you lead Boo-Boo Head to the arena to ride, your hands are sweaty and your heart is beating hard in your chest. Time to dance with your horse. Not surprisingly, Boo-Boo Head is pretty tense and spooky during your ride, which consisted of three loops around the arena ... at the walk. You consider whether tennis might be a better hobby.

Everyone deals with fear differently. To successfully salvage your dressage journey from the jaws of fear, you must at some point acknowledge its existence. Looking fear square in the eye, forgiving yourself for being fearful and making peace with your horse is half the battle.

You might wonder about the other half of the battle? Move out of the fearful dressage barn and find a really fun Western trail-riding barn! That's right, slap a big, old Western saddle on Boo-Boo Head, grab the horn and go on a *trail ride*! Don't forget to have a few glasses of wine before you head out. Remember you are, at heart, a dressage rider and beer, except expensive imported varieties, is not your beverage of choice! After a while, you are having fun again. Only then may you continue with your dressage journey.

A Truly Awful Trail Ride and My Great Fall

I am one of those lucky individuals blessed with a "Velcro® butt" in the saddle. Unfortunately, this quality has done nothing to assist me in my dressage journey. In fact, as time goes on, I suspect this quality actually hinders the development of my perfect dressage seat. At the first hint of trouble, my legs clamp like iron around my horse's sides, a legacy of my Hack Stable Queen days. I believe I would need about a solid year of daily, three-hour long lunge lessons to relax the natural "vise grip" position of my legs. Sad to say, this is not in my budget.

However, I do take considerable pride in my "stick-on" ability, even as I have entered my 4th decade. I've been guilty of looking down my nose at some of my dressage acquaintances because of their fearfulness and occasional tumbles. But you know the saying, "Pride goeth before the fall"? So true.

But before the story of "My Great Fall," there was a story that came before it. On my 40th birthday, my daughter and I trailered our magnificent "Gray Ponies" down to a friend's barn for a celebratory trail ride in honor of my great milestone. Kat and I go on frequent trail rides together at home and have participated in several pace events. Truly, these have been some of the most memorable rides I've had, cantering along side by side with my daughter across the fields. We do proceed with certain caution befitting my age and her skill level; foxhunting, for instance, is not in the foreseeable future. But we do ride out with a certain sense of fun and carefree spirit.

And so off we went, with perfect confidence to enjoy a trail ride away from home. There were several riders who joined us on my birthday ride; ladies I've never ridden with before. All were perfectly competent riders mounted on reasonably sensible horses. We set off, about seven of us in all, to enjoy the brisk fall day.

Quickly, though, it became apparent that some of these ladies were quite nervous. We were admonished to keep to a walk, because up ahead was the sight of recent deer kill, something that scared the horses. We all duly shortened our reins and tightened our legs, and sure enough, our horses were scared when we passed the deer kill site. There were many such potential disaster areas during this ride, and each was pointed out well in advance.

I have never had a less enjoyable trail ride. TFO became increasingly nervous, and so did I. Worse, my daughter was likewise infected by the atmosphere of fear. Soon, Chico was jumping around nervously. Now I was worried about Kat's safety as well as my own. Kat finally turned to me in frustration and asked if we could please trot already! Kids do have a way of seeing right to the heart of a matter.

It was a light bulb moment for me. After much hand-wringing from the group, Kat and I ever so carefully extricated ourselves and trotted off along some side paths. We eventually came upon some lovely logs. I asked the group to stop (it was my birthday after all), and Kat and I took turns jumping over these small, inviting logs. In this way, TFO and Chico settled down and we survived the ride without being totally undone by fear. It was an interesting lesson to be sure.

My second story regarding fear is about "My Great Fall." My comeuppance came when I agreed to ride, of all things, a 17.2-plus hand Percheron gelding for a gentleman who boards at my barn. This was truly comical! This horse, Seth, hasn't been in regular work for years. I needed a step ladder, literally, to groom and tack him up. My fellow barnmates were in stitches watching my attempts to get the bridle on this massive animal. I'd climb halfway up the step ladder, try to get the bit in his mouth and then start cussing as he took a half-step away. I'd move the step ladder after him and begin the process again.

I'll admit I was a bit nervous about riding Seth. When I finally mounted, it was like being astride an enormous couch. My legs barely reached the bottom of the saddle. But, relatively speaking, our first ride went well. There were no great expectations of fine equitation here. Just walk and trot around the ring a couple times. By the time I finished, I was having a great time, and all my barnmates were duly impressed.

The next day, I looked forward to riding Seth again. After the same, rather humiliating grooming and tacking up session, off we lumbered to the ring. I mounted and set off with a great deal more confidence this time. Probably my first mistake. After a suitable time walking, I asked Seth to trot off. He decided, suddenly, he was afraid of the mounting block and swerved away. "Oh no," says I! "Oh yes," says Seth! Well, leave it to me to get in a pissing match with a somewhat stubborn, 2,600 pound, almost-18-hand, Percheron gelding!

That's right, Seth launched into a series of bucks! Well, it could have been a series of bucks, but it only took the first one to send me sailing. Never in my life have I experienced such a sensation of the earth literally quaking. There was absolutely no way I could ride out that enormous buck. Airborne I went! And then the falling part: It took a long, long time to reach the ground. Despite my best attempt to twist and land on my feet, I misjudged the landing part by several feet and picked up amazing velocity on my way to Mother Earth. Yes, down I fell, hitting the ground hard with my back and neck.

It hurt—a lot. However, so did my Irish pride! I jumped to my feet rather quickly, I'm proud to say. Of course, everyone who witnessed my comeuppance was in a tizzy, asking if I was OK. I brushed off their concerns and set about retrieving the great, ugly, evil beast! My arms and legs were shaking as I led the formerly benign Seth to the mounting block. I remounted as quickly as my quivering limbs allowed and proceeded to walk the hulking demon animal about the ring. I didn't quit until I got one more trot. It was only halfway around the ring, but it was enough to salvage my wounded pride.

I rode Seth one more time after that, again for the sake of my pride, then suggested the owner find someone else to school him. It took a long, long time to recover from the aches in my back and neck from that fall. The next time I rode TFO, I mounted him with grateful ease. TFO is just under 15 hands, a very suitable size for my own 5 foot 1 inch frame. But I proceeded with a great deal more caution than usual, even with TFO. And I discovered a great deal more empathy for my dressage acquaintances, struggling to recoup both physically and mentally from their own nasty spills. ■

Frustration

"When I work with clients, the first and foremost item at the top of the list is, "Leave the world behind." When you head for your horse, leave the troubles of your daily life behind at the house. No kids, no bills, no bickering with the significant other, no car trouble, no nothing is brought with you. The reason for this philosophy is quite simple, the horse is extremely sensitive to your emotional and mental state. We humans have too many short circuits going on in the brain all the time, and horses just do not want that kind of space around them. With all *that being said, it is your state of mind and HEART that is the controlling factor when engaging with the horse. Patience is the greatest lesson you can learn ...* **"**

spirithorse, "How do you maintain your patience?" 1/4/04, UDBB

Frustration is yet another one of those ugly emotions you'll be dealing with on a first name basis along your dressage journey. Of course, we are all grown-ups here. We've dealt with frustration and have come to terms with it in our adult lives. It's not the end of the world, right?

Grocery Shopping

Take for instance, grocery shopping. This is an onerous chore squeezed in to your precious weekend. You've made your list, cut your coupons and are ready to go. Only you discover that you have laundry detergent on your list, and your coupon for Tide with Bleach has expired. From experience, you know the pimply-faced young checkout clerks at the store will bust you, so you toss the offending coupon away. Frustrating, but oh well!

As you set off, you discover your gas tank is on empty, so you must stop to get gas first, which takes a long time in your big SUV. Again, frustrating—but certainly not the end of the world! You suppress those dark thoughts about the impending global oil shortage and the Middle East crisis while you're waiting for your tank to fill. Filling the tank of this gas hog will take a long time, so to pass the time, you decide to balance your checkbook. It is then you realize you've forgotten (lost?) your checkbook and have to tap your ATM card before you can go grocery shopping. Since it's a Saturday morning, you end up waiting in line for another half hour to get some "quick" cash. Your eyelids are starting to twitch.

Finally, just as you pull into the parking lot of the grocery store, you are cut off by the assisted living center van. Oh God, you groan inwardly—a store full of blue-hairs in walkers and wheelchairs! Now you'll be mowing down senior citizens in the aisles as you attempt to expedite your shopping. Your jaw is clenched at this point. At the rate this is going, you won't have time to ride Boo-Boo Head this afternoon! Nevertheless, you race through the store, dodging the elderly and infirmed with practiced skill and remember to pick up all the ingredients to make a nice lasagna dinner for tonight. So by the time you get home from your grocery shopping—three hours later—you are frustrated and cranky. It's all a part of life. No big deal!

"Dancing" with Your Horse

You will experience the same snowballing effects of frustration while riding your horse. As you are already two hours behind schedule, you rush frantically to the barn. At last its time to ride Boo-Boo Head! Once there, you discover Boo-Boo Head has strategically chosen this time to be in the north 40 of the pasture. As you grab his halter and get ready to take a hike, the barn owner corners you and hands you a bill for repairs to the fencing Boo-Boo Head damaged last week while trying to make introductions with the sexy new boarder—a mare in season. OK, you sigh, frustrated, yet still undeterred from your mission.

You stuff the bill in your pocket and proceed to trek three miles, picking through mud and manure, to catch the great Romeo. Once you reach him, huffing and puffing, you are sure he's laughing at you. He meets you—the last three steps—to get his carrot. Of course, he isn't wearing his blanket and has rolled vigorously in the mud—on both sides—while paying special attention to rubbing his face in the muck. Obviously, Boo-Boo Head found a way to relieve his pent-up romantic aspirations.

You mentally calculate the time required to get Boo-Boo Head suitably groomed as you make the three-mile trek back to the barn. Of course, you are leading Boo-Boo Head because God forbid you should swing up on him bareback and let him carry you! You are mentally rearranging your dinner plans at this point. Instead of a nice lasagna dinner, hot dogs will do. Then you fret: Did you remember to pick up hot dog buns while shopping? No matter, just slap the dog on a piece of bread, you decide. This will leave approximately 20 minutes to actually ride Boo-Boo Head.

So, finally, back at the barn and with one eye on the clock, you proceed to groom the mud off Boo-Boo Head as quickly as possible. Your eyelid is twitching again. For some unknown reason, Boo-Boo Head is quite ticklish and jumpy as you groom him with hard, quick strokes of the brush. You tell him sternly, more than once, to stand still. Twitch, twitch!

The fourth time he jumps about, you give him a firm smack on the butt. With that, Boo-Boo Head leaps forward and breaks the crossties. Son of a b****! It takes a while to catch him, as he seems to be regarding you with a great deal of fear (the ingrate) as you run after him, screaming and cursing. You do end up catching him after enlisting three of your barnmates to help run him into a corner with lunge whips.

Back in the crossties, you finish tacking up the wild-eyed Boo-Boo Head who watches bug-eyed as you strap on your spurs and pick up your whip. Yes, finally, you are ready to ride. You're way behind schedule now, but decide to skip dinner altogether. You're on a diet anyway, and both lasagna and hot dogs are so fattening! Yes, now at last, its time to dance with your horse.

Rage

> "But the biggest enemy to the partnership of dressage is impatience and the human nature to dominate other creatures. To reach a good partnership, the rider must control himself before controlling his horse."
> **Walter Zettl, Dressage in Harmony**

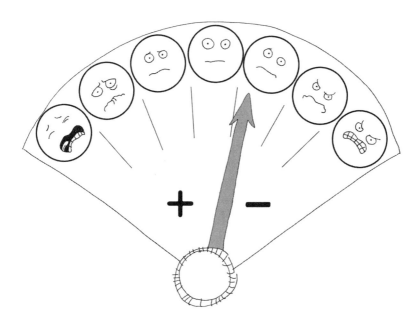

Dressage Emotion Guage

Yes, you can probably see where all this fear and frustration is leading. That's right, you got it—rage—the final and ugliest of our triumvirate of dark emotions. As you lead the wild-eyed Boo-Boo Head to the arena, you now have 10 minutes to ride. You are beyond frustrated!

You review in your mind the absolute essentials you need to cover in this session while your stomach is growling from hunger and you think of all the weight you need to lose and wonder where you lost your checkbook. Forget Zen! Forget the Generally Accepted Training Pyramid and the all-important rhythm and relaxation! Now it's time to get On the Bit!

Suffice it say, your ride does not go well. Boo-Boo Head is tense and uncooperative, and before long you are cursing and swearing, yanking and cranking and, generally, neither of you is having a very good time. As you pull back on the reins, you are thinking of all the harsh admonishments from your trainers and from the dressage books about pulling back on the reins. Soon you feel guilty and hungry and mad; truly a bad combination.

You end up riding Boo-Boo Head for 45 minutes over your allotted 10 minutes. He still won't get the left lead canter. You finally end the miserable session, spent from all this negative emotion, despairing of ever achieving On the Bit and moving out of Intro into Training Level.

You go home, open up a bag of potato chips, pour a glass of wine and pop in your favorite video—Tape 18: Reiner Klimke riding a Grand Prix Freestyle on Alerich. One day this will be you!

Poor, Dear Lucy

I've been at the same boarding barn for several years now. I love it. It's a small, self-care barn on a beautiful estate. The owner's wife, Lucy, is a lovely woman, inside and out. She had ridden hunters in her youth and has long retired from actual riding. Month after month, year after year, Lucy has strolled past the ring, back and forth to the barn, and observed my many frantic attempts at dressage. That's right, Lucy has seen them all—Chad, Gus, Chico and TFO.

I know she's puzzled, especially when she sees some of my more bizarre efforts, like riding in side reins. She's also had the misfortune to witness my more temperamental moments. Nonetheless, she always has a sweet smile and an encouraging word for me—bless her! I'm sure she sneaks out after I've gone to give my poor horses much deserved apples for their tolerance. Ah, dressage! Lucy just doesn't understand—she's one of those who believe riding should be an enjoyable endeavor! ■

CHAPTER SEVEN
A Look on the Lighter Side (?)

You are, no doubt, totally despairing at this point, having completed your "walk on the dark side." Poor Boo-Boo Head, you are thinking. Perhaps it would be better to forget dressage and take up tennis? But take heart, there is a lighter side to your journey— really—there is!

Well, perhaps there is. Let's take a stroll and review some of the more ridiculous aspects of this somber endeavor. Laughter is, after all, the best medicine. Let's look some "weighty" matters—like how we stuff ourselves into those ridiculous riding breeches—and perhaps discuss the relative qualities of both types of Dressage Queens. And let's not forget, speaking of size, how size does matter—the size of your horse, that is.

Come, come. Let's stop despairing.

Weighty Matters

*"Some people are 'designed' to be riders, runners, bas-
ketball players, etc. This doesn't mean they will be, it just
means they have a head start on the rest of us should
they decide to maximize their talent with hard work and
training. If you think about the origins of dressage, that
is, as a military activity, is it surprising that a lean, male,
athletic body has natural advantages?"*
Peter Guy, "How much natural talent?" 7/27/03, UDBB

OK, what is up with riding attire? Surely we are all aware that
obesity in the United States has soared to epidemic proportions. And
even if we are not technically "obese," the percentage of moderate-
ly overweight people—those who are pleasantly plump—has been
growing by leaps and bounds. Furthermore—not to beat a dead
horse—surely we had enough of that with poor Boo-Boo Head—
but we've concluded that dressage riders are composed of primarily
middle class, middle-aged white women.

We all know what happens when we reach middle age—that's
right—we lose our sylph-like, girlish form (if we ever had one to
begin with), and our hips, thighs and stomach begin their inevitable
expansion. We lose the battle against gravity as our chins, breasts and
buttocks begin their predictable droop downward.

Long ago, in the dark ages, before the dreaded Baby Boom era, this
was an honorable part of the aging process. But no more! Unlike our
grandmothers, we live in a dismaying time where it is incumbent

upon us to fight nature's way and maintain ourselves in model-like svelteness. Most of us fail.

Are we not glued to Oprah's ongoing battle with weight? One year she's trim and stylish, and then we watch with gleeful vindictiveness as her clothing size inches upwards. Then we watch show after show of her battles to defeat the form nature intended for her. Deep down we hope she fails so we don't feel so bad. And isn't Oprah a billionaire? She has all the money in the world to hire personal fitness trainers and dieticians to support her in her battle! No doubt, Oprah's enduring popularity is because, half the time, she does fail in her battles against weight. How can you not love her, clever girl?

Many strategies have been developed to help disguise our growing proportions as we age. The most time-honored is strategically wearing our clothing to hide some of our more glaring conformation faults. The biggest fashion no-no is wearing skin tight, form fitting attire. This is entirely the realm of our svelte 20-something sisters— not for the average middle-aged woman.

So what is up with those riding breeches? That's right, for the sake of this "art form" we are forced to wear the most humiliating clothing ever designed to make us feel bad—riding breeches! Skin tight, Lycra-enhanced material that hugs every lump and bump of our thighs, butts and stomachs! Really, is this some cruel joke?

Have you ever asked yourself, "Why must I wear riding breeches in order to correctly ride dressage? Isn't my self-esteem battered enough?" And even more excruciating—we must wear *white* riding breeches in the show ring! Well, technically the rules state *light* colored breeches are required. But hey, we all know that white is the not-to-be-broken unspoken rule. At least we can wear those relatively concealing black breeches while schooling at home. But at shows, white is mandatory! I ask you, how much more wretched can this get?

Think about this: How many times have you hovered at your front door making sure your neighbors were out of sight before dashing to your car, because you're dressed to ride? Have you not about swooned in dismay when you've been spotted retrieving your mail after coming home from the barn, again, because you are dressed to ride? You know your neighbors are laughing at you, and you have been the source of endless discussion regarding your—ahem—expansive buttocks!

To put riding breeches into perspective, it is helpful to look at some history here. It wasn't until the United States Cavalry (using horses, that is) officially disbanded—after that great equestrian milestone, World War II—that women entered the world of recreational riding in force. As you now understand, prior to this time, dressage was the domain of military schools and secret horse societies. As we all know, those activities were, and are, dominated by men.

The significance of this is that riding breeches were designed for men—men who are fit for active military duty or from years of grueling barn work. These men generally do not have to deal with issues of spreading thighs, butts and stomachs. Cellulite is not the bane of their existence.

And let's face it; riding breeches only look good on the one percent of female riders who are actually built like these military men—in that they have no thighs, butts or stomachs. Those riders are, of course, the really successful riders. A quick, pictorial study of the World Equestrian Games results will reveal that all the successful women riders are built along the same lines—none of them have butts, thighs or stomachs to speak of. When you open your latest sales catalog from Dover or Dressage Extensions, check out the women posing in riding breeches. That's right, you won't find any thighs, butts or stomachs on them either. Of course, these women aren't riders. Worse, they are models.

This should not dissuade us—the majority of dressage riders—from taking a stand. Until someone comes up with a perfectly valid reason why we must wear riding breeches in order to correctly ride dressage, why not wear a pair of sweats? Sweats are comfortable. Perhaps not stylish, but relative to riding breeches, enough said! And furthermore, why isn't there a line of "easy-fit" riding breeches—like the way blue jeans are designed these days? Designed to be more "forgiving" in the thigh, butt and stomach? There is a fortune to be made here!

This is truly one of the times it is worthwhile to think "outside the box." Rather than just submit quietly to this horrid tradition, remember that it is your dollars that support dressage in the United States. Take a stand! Tell them you won't take it anymore! Either design a more flattering style of riding breeches, or allow us to wear sweats—dark colored sweats, no less—while riding and showing dressage!

Forget about the USDF's attempts at certifying qualified dressage trainers. The first step to feeling better about your dressage journey is to take up the cause of banning riding breeches from competitions! Inundate the USDF with letters and petitions! Start a grass roots campaign at your Group Member Organization (GMO). Design a Web site to support the cause! Let them feel your wrath! You are the backbone of the dressage industry, and you can make a difference!

The Anatomy of the Dressage Queen

"Hanging out on both coasts (USA) and in Europe, I've met and even admired a number of DQs. Many are humorous, generous and good companions. (Practiced social skills.) Most of 'em can actually ride. (All that good nutrition, exercise and massage builds a tight body.) Some ride VERY well and have a good insight into what the horse needs, how to get him to give his best. (All that expensive training with the very best trainers actually takes hold.) A few can/have ridden broncs. All this while wearing diamonds and looking gorgeous—and having someone to do the scut work for you. Sigh! It really grinds my gears!"
SmithsonLM, "Can Dressage Queens Ride?" 11/14/03, UDBB

No book about dressage could ever be complete without discussing the relative merits of our reigning divas—The Dressage Queens, or as they are more simply known, DQs. The real DQs, you see, look fabulous in riding breeches, regardless of their riding ability. It is for this reason—above all—that DQs are universally despised by Intro and Training Level riders. Yes, we are the ones who generally require easy-fit riding breeches and are currently launching a campaign to end the wearing of these abhorrent items.

And who is it that stands in our way? The DQs, that's who. We can forgive a lot—like the fact they have the best trainers and the most expensive horses. We can accept the fact that they own six homes here and abroad. We can forgive them their money and their jewelry and their exotic vacations. We can even forgive their occasional arrogant outbursts—because we secretly admire and are in awe of them.

Dressage Queen

But we can't forgive them for looking good in riding breeches. We understand, at the most primal level, that with their money and influence, DQs stand between us and the end of wearing riding breeches. They have invested their entire lives into perfecting their svelte form. Thousands and thousands of dollars worth of plastic surgery and liposuction, and hours and hours of strenuous daily exercises have gone into the shaping of those fit, middle-age bodies. They've endured pain and suffering of Olympic proportions. What is their reward? Looking good in riding breeches!

Oh no! Don't expect the campaign to end the wearing of riding breeches to go easily! Not with the DQs standing between us and our greatest wish. It is here that the caste system in the United States—a rarely discussed or acknowledged phenomenon in our democracy—will become fully engaged. The DQs are, of course, the blue-blooded Brahmins of our caste system. Given the many sacrifices they have laid on the alter of slimness, they have a vested interest in keeping riding breeches a mandatory prerequisite to riding dressage. Yes, it could shape up to be a battle of epic proportions, much like the size of our ever-expanding butts!

The Quest for Physical Fitness

"*Joining the choir here—pilates is amazing. It's like dressage for people. Same ideas and theories, and the same end goal of the perfectly supple, even, ideally muscled athlete.*"

twotempi01, "Pilates for riders," 7/7/03, UDBB

Yes, the battle to end the wearing of riding breeches looks to be a long, uphill struggle. In the meantime, the average dressage rider will no doubt venture down some side roads in an attempt to combine weight loss with improving riding skills. You will acquire an entire sub-library to your dressage books regarding the physical and mental fitness of the dressage rider.

While you are to be admired for actually participating in regular exercise, riding, unfortunately, will not be enough to maintain the fitness you need to be a dressage rider. As discussed in Chapter Four: "Dressage Movements," one must be able to sustain a great deal of pain to sit the trot. This requires a certain physical strength. Riding the sitting trot four or five days a week is not enough, ironically, to develop the strength to sit the trot. It figures! Therefore, you must branch out into other physical fitness endeavors.

It is believed that dressage riders have driven the upsurge in the popularity of pilates. Most riders started with yoga only to realize that yoga just isn't physically demanding enough to meet our requirements. Sure, all that mental focus stuff is good, and at first you think yoga is the answer. But quickly it becomes apparent that yoga isn't excruciating enough to satisfy the masochistic tendencies of dressage riders.

That's right, the bar keeps rising, and yoga won't be sufficient for you to develop your "core strength." Military men, Dressage Queens and female Olympic riders have "core strength." It has something to do with *not* having thighs, butts or stomachs. Yes, this is another dirty little secret in the dressage world, like the half halt (again, please see Chapter Four: Dressage Movements).

But as you are painfully aware, dressage riders are totally obsessed with trying to correctly ride dressage, and no path is left unexplored in our quest for the perfect 20-meter circle. So after practicing your best gentle yoga poses for a while, you will move on to pilates. Pilates is really painful because it focuses on developing "core strength." Much like dressage itself, correctly learning pilates requires a single minded, lifelong dedication. In its purist form, pilates utilizes frightening looking contraptions that rival "The Rack" used in the Spanish Inquisition. When you stumble upon these, you know you've come to the right place to augment your dressage journey! This is going to hurt! Perfect!

Unfortunately, most of us can't afford to buy the proper torture instruments used in pilates. The bulk of our discretionary funds are spent on maintaining the upscale lifestyle of our dressage horses. This is the priority, after all. So, we content ourselves with pilates mat classes given at the local YMCA, sans the torture chamber accoutrements. It's still pretty painful with lots of bizarre abdominal-focused exercises, but it's simply not enough to reduce our thighs, butts and stomachs to develop proper "core strength." However, you can be proud of the great strides you've made in firming up the previously gelatin-like mass of your thighs, butt and stomach. Great big "atta girl"!

The Quest for Mental Fitness

"*I have spent the last four years doing "horsemanship" work—or so I thought. But the most significant changes have happened in me internally. I finally started to realize*

that … it is about ALL relationships, teaching us to "con-
nect," and "let go" emotionally, detach and take respon-
sibility for our contributions in these relationships—bad
and good. I never expected this part—I just wanted to
"do dressage!" Whoa—all this sounds like therapist talk.
Then I realized, really good horsemanship training is bet-
ter than therapy because you get to practice the rela-
tionship interaction and have the immediate feedback of
a coach—your horse!"
lmcgilli, "Joy in growth," 10/6/03, UDBB

You may also take heart that your time with yoga was not
wasted. While the gentle stretching of yoga was not enough to develop "core strength," you were introduced to methods of "mental
focus," which is of great value to dressage ridesr. Remember that
dressage is a spiritual journey as well as a physical one. We have
learned that the perfect 20-meter circle requires more than just
Olympic-level fitness. It also requires the mental tranquility of a
Buddhist monk! Is this not the *best* art form ever invented?

You no longer scoff at your dressage acquaintances who attend
weekly sessions with their sports psychologist. No, indeed, now you
are jealous of them. You have come to understand that the riding of
dressage mirrors your entire psychological development. Every
experience you've had, good and bad, from birth onward, is reflected
in your riding.

This is why, you see, you cannot get the left lead canter. Because you
haven't forgiven your mother for forbidding you to wear makeup
when you were 12 years old! You were the only girl at the seventh

grade dance without blue eye shadow and dayglo bubble gum lipstick. Remember how you clung to the auditorium walls, mortified with embarrassment? Deeply scarring memories like this are what inhibit the development of your dressage abilities. Just as you start to focus on picking up the canter, your mind performs a flashback to that horrifying seventh grade dance, and your concentration is lost.

Yes, you begin to delve into these long-suppressed memories in your quest for the perfect 20-meter circle. Only by resolving these angst-filled events will you have the necessary focus to engage the outside hind leg, rather than the inside fore, to achieve the correct lead at the canter.

So you will begin to explore more esoteric disciplines in your quest for the perfect 20-meter circle. Yoga is just a start. Next, you explore Zen and, before long, you are able to spout profound sayings about peace on earth and the half halt, even though you still can't perform a half halt and haven't a clue about the current state of world! Regardless, you've grown in maturity and wisdom, thanks to your quest for mental fitness, and you now enjoy a much better relationship with your mother. See that!

Understanding the True Nature of Railbirds

There is another benefit to your new mental fitness—the ability to better deal with the dreaded "railbirds." You know who I'm speaking about—those catty women who gather at the edges of the arena and exchange vicious remarks about your riding ability and how you look in riding breeches. Railbirds exist in all equestrian disciplines, but given the advanced intellectual capabilities of dressage riders, dressage railbirds are truly among the worst.

Yes remember, middle-aged women, whom, by nature of their sex and maturity, are the most skilled at skewering their peers with razor-sharp precision, dominate dressage. Throughout the ages, women have used this time-honored method to deal with rivals, given the female disdain for fisticuffs. This skill has been further honed by an eternity of political, social and economic inequity. One should never underestimate the truly vicious capabilities of middle-aged women. In the hands of dressage riders, this capacity for vicious-ness is a weapon wielded with deadly accuracy.

Of course, you are not one of them. You are simply a victim of these vicious women who never miss an opportunity to point out the many times you jerked back on the reins. They discuss your woeful dressage failings behind your back with maniacal glee. The truly gift-ed will commiserate with you to your face and then get out the dag-gers when your back is turned. Indeed, these women duly dissect every pound you gained over the Thanksgiving-to-Christmas binge fest, since it is painfully obvious when you're wearing your riding breeches—even the black pair.

But given your new metaphysical awareness, you no longer indulge in this negative "gossip-mongering." It creates a dark aura around your Zen-state, thereby interrupting your attempts to engage the outside hind, rather than the inside fore, in obtaining the correct lead canter. No, you save your spiritual cleansing for important issues, like the woman at your barn who is truly awful. Clearly, her failings, unlike yours, are so glaring that it is your duty to share your opinion with your dressage acquaintances. It is almost noble to point out this woman's many failings.

This is not the same, you see, as being an embittered "railbird." You are to be congratulated, instead, for attempting to point out this woman's atrocious riding skills. After all, it is incumbent upon you to uphold the high standards of purity in this art form called dressage. You, unlike them, are one of good guys. Indeed, all your efforts at mental fitness have paid off, unlike your somewhat uneven results at physical fitness. This is another benefit derived from your dressage journey.

Comparative Anatomy—The Other Dressage Queens

> **"**Funny, until the U.S. Cavalry was mechanized in 1949, horses were a GUY thing. It only became a 'sissy' sport once women took it over. And this is not the women's fault, but the other men who created the generalization.**"**
> **Mark Susol, "Men and Lessons," 1/21/04, UDBB**

Here is an interesting phenomenon regarding dressage. Since the collapse of the U.S. Cavalry at the end of WWII, and the huge influx of women into the world of recreational riding, suddenly riding, in general, and dressage, in particular, is a "sissy" sport. No self-respecting man would be caught dead riding dressage. "What? Ride in a sandbox and wear those tight, white breeches?" they exclaim with horror!

Hey, it's OK for a man to pull on his Wrangler jeans and rope some steer from his rugged western saddle. After all, most of us were weaned on images of the "Marlboro Man." If, heaven forbid, a man should ride in the sissy English style, well, he'd better be jumping some pretty substantial fences. Foxhunting and polo—more extreme horse sports—also pass the male definition of what is suitably macho.

But dressage? Those men who do brave the esoteric world of dressage are labeled—you've got it—the "other" dressage queens. Oh yes, they lisp, "I look good," as they model their snug white breeches in front of their full-length mirror and debate the addition of a pair of socks to enhance their—ahem—profile. The clichés and jokes regarding men and dressage are endless.

Oh, the irony—the superb irony! Dressage—the ultimate expression of equestrian accomplishment—was developed because the horse was the single, most potent piece of military armament! Ha, ha, ha! Women are quietly, yet hysterically, laughing at this sudden male disdain for the dressage. What is the capriole, after all, but a superb war maneuver whereby the horse kicks the crap out of some hapless enemy about to slay you with a sword?

Yes, it is both puzzling yet inevitable that dressage—grounded firmly and thoroughly in the art of war—should now be considered the bastion of the "other dressage queens." Yet further proof that, as many studies have concluded, the typical gay man has both a keener fashion sense and a higher I.Q. than the average heterosexual male. Certainly, something women understand while "real" men mock—

when they manage to drag their attention away from watching the football game—a sport where men run around wearing snug white breeches!

Size Does Matter— A Horse That Fits

Since we are pursuing such a plethora of weighty topics, now might be a good time to discuss that burning topic: Does size matter? Again, I must beseech you to pull your mind out of gutter—this is a dressage book! Ahem! We are discussing the size of your horse, of course. Geez!

The size of your dressage horses will go up and then back down through the course of your dressage journey. Your first (but not last) dressage horse, you see, was not big enough to keep you satisfied in the early part of your journey when you were still naive and eager. You became very envious of your dressage acquaintances who had really, really big ones. They seemed to be having much more fun than you. You gazed longingly at those big guys with their huge ... trots. "Wow," you thought. "If only I had such a *big* one, then I'd be a truly fulfilled." Size does matter, you concluded, and the bigger the better.

No doubt your second (but not last) dressage horse was the biggest one you could afford to buy. It goes without saying, especially in the culture of the United States, that size, like youth, is highly prized. You will pay a pretty penny for a really, really big one. You will spend a fortune on one that is both big *and* good-looking. You overlooked countless other flaws in your second (but not last) dressage horse because you were fixated on his size; his really big size! You fairly beamed with pride when you showed off your big guy to all your dressage friends. You were secretly smug because you knew they envied you his incredible size. You were sure you had fulfilled your every dressage dream with the big guy. You couldn't wait to sit that … trot. That really big trot!

Sadly, though, you quickly realized that you were not capable of handling his size. He was just too big for you to really enjoy him. Your rides became increasingly uncomfortable, as you fought valiantly to sit that great big … trot. After a while, his big size got downright painful.

Ah, maturity! As you continued on your journey, you realized there were more important things than just good looks and a really big size. Personality, for instance, was a previously underrated quality. Having the biggest one may be fun at first, but after a while, you begin to long for something easier and more manageable. Yes, you will eventually and correctly deduce that those really big, good-looking ones, with all their associated ego issues, are best left for younger, more athletic riders.

Alas, your next dressage horse most likely won't be so big. You will select him because he is smart, charming and has a great personality. A piece of you will always look back nostalgically on that really big one. But with your new, smaller one, you will find a comfort level that is worth the trade off. No longer will you have to suffer the spiteful jealousy of your dressage acquaintances. No longer will you have to worry about the big one's huge ego and if he truly loved you for you or secretly wished for a younger, prettier rider.

You have no such doubts with your new, smaller one. He appreciates your love. He doesn't care how you look in riding breeches. He loves you for you because he is not obsessed with how big he is and, frankly, his lack of size makes him a bit insecure. Size, you realize, isn't the most important thing. It's all about personality and a good fit. Bigger is not always better. You've learned that the hard way.

Dressage Shows

"Riding to win, or for high scores, or for the opinion of others, leads one into a strange world of external pressures that can destroy riders and horses. When the rider/artist gives up control, he gives up his only real

chance to be free. I believe that all these riders are innately aware of their deal with the devil."

Paul Belasik, *Riding Toward the Light*

The Tedium of Judging

Have you ever wondered about the scoring of dressage tests? Have you ever really sat down and wondered what it all means? For those of you Intro and Training Level riders who bravely go forth into the world of showing with much angst and nail biting, does the scoring ever make you sit back and reflect on what the heck you're getting so worked up about?

Like figure skating, dressage judging is entirely subjective. A judge sits in his box and assigns a number from 1 to 10 for each specific movement you perform in the test. A humble assistant, called the scribe, frantically jots down these numbers along with associated comments given by the judge. Scribes suffer a high degree of burnout. Like air traffic controllers, the job combines high pressure with extreme tedium. The main difference between air traffic controllers and scribes is that scribes don't get paid.

An Intro Level test is composed of 10 movements, along with four "collective" scores. Collective scores, which are general impressions of gaits, impulsion, submission and rider position, are used to pad the numbers, since there is no real dressage performed at the Intro or Training Levels.

Do you ever wonder how much judges get paid? They have the excruciating task of sitting in a little box watching test after test after test until they are cross-eyed with boredom. Most of the tests at the average dressage schooling shows are Intro and Training Level. A judge will have the good fortune to see perhaps three riders performing usually awful renditions of First Level. The other 94 riders are evenly split between Intro and Training Level. How incredibly boring is that?

The Numbers Don't Lie

> "I wish more judges would give out 40 percent scores for deplorable riding and more 80 percent scores for excellent riding. As long as 65 percent is viewed as a glass ceiling, folks getting 52 percent are going to think they're not that far behind when, in reality, they are many levels away from progressive training. Why are there so few 80 percent scores? So big deal if the best score is 75 percent. If we are judging against a defined standard that means there's 25 percent more improvement to go."
>
> **Mark Susol, "Judges are killing the dressagesport," 1/4/04, UDBB**

This is why, you see, the scores given out by dressage judges are so low. They are bored and cranky! Very rarely does one achieve higher than a C (in the 70th percentile) or D (in the 60th percentile). Even more sadly, Fs (in the 50th percentile) are quite routine. This is because riders aren't riding dressage at dressage shows. They are performing On the Bit, which is not the same as dressage, only the riders don't know it. A few judges do actually know the difference between On the Bit and dressage. They are the ones to avoid. They are even crankier than the judges who don't know the difference between On the Bit and dressage.

Fortunately, riders have proven quite adaptable. Instead of worrying about our incredibly low scores, we simply take them for granted. Instead of being upset over getting a "D," we look at it as a good thing. Scores in the 60s are entirely respectable, even admirable! Even getting marked down in the 50s is not considered the end of the world. Many of us get scores in the 50s. And what is our interpretation of this failing grade? Well, it simply means we are not yet ready to move up to the next level. That's all. There is no shame associated with scoring in the 50s. Now, a score in the 40s does result in a bit of embarrassment. That score means you need stay at home and practice some more.

And then, of course, there are those fortunate few who have actually achieved an average grade—a C. That's right, how remarkable is our ability to rationalize poor grades, I ask you? For an Intro or Training Level rider to receive a score in the 70th percentile is dressage nirvana! You are hailed a conquering hero—at first. This is because a score in 70s means it's well past time for you to move on to the next level. If you achieve more than one score in the 70s, you are either a score-mongering loiterer or unfairly mounted on a Grand Prix schoolmaster! You may receive a score of 70 only once or twice before the audience begins pelting you with rotten fruit as you exit the arena.

These are some things to ponder while you're meditating to enhance your dressage journey. There is only one saving grace in the entire grading system. The upper level riders are basically achieving the same grades as the Intro and Training Level riders! That's right, the guys in the big leagues are getting 60s and 70s as well. They don't very often get failing scores though, and there are a few that actually achieve 80s. These are, not surprisingly, usually the Dutch and German riders. Intro and Training Level riders can take some comfort in this. Evidently, these top riders are barely capable of breaking a B, let alone getting on the honor roll. It does make one suspect that the entire dressage system is geared towards battering one's self esteem. Remember, you gave up trail riding for this abuse.

The Great 76.5

Yes, this is the section you have all been waiting for! This is the story of 76.5 percent. My crowning score at Intro Level with TFO! The pinnacle of my dressage career! Yes, indeed, I earned a C on a walk/trot test and thought I'd just about died and gone to heaven! For that forever cherished, yet brief, moment, every doubt I ever had regarding my riding ability vanished! But wait, let's back up. Before 76.5 percent, I actually scored a 75.5 percent and was sure things could never get better.

Yes, it all started with 75.5. I had only shown TFO a handful of times prior to 75.5. We debuted, miserably, at Training Level, with scores in the low 50s, and that was a gift from the judge, to be sure. Actually, I was quite proud of our first test. As we trotted down the long side, preparing for a canter depart, TFO noticed there were real, live people in the judge's box! Next thing I knew, instead of a lovely canter depart, we were whipped around at lightening speed and bolting off in the opposite direction!

Again, this is where my illustrious background as a Hack Stable Queen came in handy. Just as quick, I executed a perfect pulley rein, about-face maneuver that is one of my specialties. Yes, all in the blink of an eye we were back on track. Of course, TFO was nowhere near being On the Bit but, regardless, I was quite proud of finishing that test! I did conclude, however, that we should stand down to Intro Level until TFO had a little more seasoning.

In the meantime, I switched trainers, yet again. This time I chose a big name trainer. How cool is this guy—I mean he's a really, really big name. He has written books! And yet he was completely gracious about taking on a "nobody" Intro/Training Level student with a young, green horse. For once, I simply shut my eyes and put my faith in a trainer without second-guessing. Just do it, I thought. This is a big name trainer, for heaven's sake!

And so, after starting with once-a-month lessons with my big name trainer, TFO and I achieved 75.5. Wow, you might think! There is the answer! Just ride with a big name trainer! No—I'm sorry to say—that is not the simple answer. I only got out of my big name trainer what I was ready to learn, which had very much to do with all the trainers and horses that preceded him. I still can't perform a decent shoulder-in, but I'm much better at On the Bit. And I'm talking about Intro Level, for heaven's sake.

The real reason I scored 75.5 was because it was a rare evening schooling show, in the middle of the summer. As such, I had two glasses of buzz-inducing wine while waiting for my turn to perform. That's right. It was the all-important cocktail hour and not to be missed! I was, shall we say, "relaxed"! What a miraculous transformation in my formerly "hot tamale" Andalusian! For once, he wasn't tense and spooky. No, quite the opposite, our warm-up was a thing of beauty. Cool, I remember thinking. When the time came to do our Intro test, I sailed in very calmly. When I completed the test, I didn't feel we had achieved anything too remarkable. Really. I thought, oh that was nice—pleasant, even. What a good boy, TFO! Doo-da-doo ... Off to the trailer to untack.

My husband was with me on this great night. Yes, I have an amazingly wonderful, supportive dressage husband, certainly of the caliber of the great Brian McKeown, author of the very first (but not last) funny dressage book, Enter at A, Laughing. In his best sup-portive fashion, my husband rolled his eyes, handed me yet another glass of wine and went to pick up my test while I cooed and fussed over my beloved TFO. And there it was—75.5 and high score champion of the show. Was the judge drinking, too, we all wondered? Really, who cares! Being utterly uncool—I literally jumped up and down, shrieking with delight, and then had another glass of wine!

I mean how funny is that? It was definitely worth the hangover. We are, without a doubt, our own worst enemies when it comes to dressage. I could cite you chapter and verse about TFO being so incredibly difficult to ride. And yet, it all comes down to the fact that it is my behavior that makes him that way. TFO is highly intelligent, very proud and very much in tune to my emotions. Really, think carefully before getting an Andalusian, or a Nokota, for that matter. They have the ability to take you to heights of glory or to the bottom of the abyss, and it's all of your own creation. Golly, isn't this just the best art form every invented?

Having achieved 75.5, I went on to score 76.5 at our next show, at Intro of course. And, I hasten to add, without the alcoholic inducement, lest you mistake me for one of those rowdy eventers or foxhunters! That's not to say I wasn't tempted to take a nip or two, but it was much too early, even for me, at 8 a.m. in the morning! No, I was my normal sober and white-knuckled self. We had our usual perfectly horrid warm-up—but TFO unaccountably retained some of the serenity of our previous show when he entered the arena to be judged. He does love to show off that mane and tail!

Ironically, our scores in the 70s have been routinely accompanied by exhortations from the judges, my fellow competitors and even the girl handing out the test scores, that it is "time to move up." Really! It was even written on the comments on the test! Time to move up. I actually argued with a judge, like, "Have you seen this horse in the warm-up arena? He's as fruity as a loon! We can't get the left lead canter. And you think it's time to move up to Training Level? I have more than 30 years of riding experience, and you think it's time to try the canter???"

Really, those comments make me so angry I sometimes contemplate moving back to the Other School where the walk/trot is proudly practiced for years and years. Until I realized I have to go back to learning the four-track shoulder-in. Hence my strategy of moving to Elementary Level combined tests. Time to move up, indeed!

The only accolade I received from my big name trainer, who is so much more highly evolved than I ever hope to be, was the following priceless comment. Upon hearing my triumphant accomplishment at Intro Level dressage, my big name trainer, who routinely performs the piaffe and levade, muttered under his breath, eyebrows raised, "Huh. Sometimes even the blind squirrel gets the nut."

How true! I howled with laughter the entire ride home! How funny is this thing we call dressage? How funny indeed! ∎

CHAPTER EIGHT
Reflections on the True Meaning of Dressage

So here at last we reach the final stage of our *Survival Guide* journey. To be sure, it has been a tumultuous, angst-filled journey. At this point, you must be wondering why we subject ourselves to this endlessly frustrating, bittersweet endeavor. Why indeed?

That's right, dancing effortlessly across the sand arena with your horse remains as distant as the stars, despite your best efforts. You have learned early on that you are the source of all your horse's problems. You've poured thousands and thousands of dollars into your journey to be taught this ironic fact. Your self-esteem has plummeted into that 20 by 60 meter arena more times than you care to remember.

And yet, you keep pulling yourself back up, dusting yourself off and continuing on. Why? What is it about dressage, anyway? Here in our final discussion, let us talk seriously about the magic and mystique of this elusive art form. Shall we?

Because, Sometimes, Even the Blind Squirrel Gets the Nut

> **"**And then there are those rides you create entirely by yourself, that are pure magic, and you still don't know how you did it, and you spend the rest of your life trying to do it again ...When we have these occasional glimpses of magic, it keeps us trying incessantly, never knowing when it will happen again.**"**
>
> **goneriding, 11/5/03, "Magic," UDBB**

In its cruel way, dressage occasionally opens a window of understanding to the always-struggling dressage rider. You will, from the very beginning, get flashes of what it is meant to be. Your first or second (but not last) horse will, at the oddest moments, offer you real dressage.

You will find yourself sitting centered and his back will lift, he will be both forward and light, and On the Bit. You power down the centerline and achieve a brilliant, straight leg yield by merely turning your head slightly. You hit the rail and ask for the canter and are rewarded with a surge of powerfully slow, exquisite strides. You halt, square, at C through no physical effort—merely by a thought—then go forward into a gorgeous trot without changing a molecule of your body.

You, most likely, have no idea how you created this moment. By the time you reach A, alas, it is gone. But for those brief strides, you are a centaur. Like watching a train as it wrecks—sliding off its tracks—everything goes in slow motion. Every horse you have ridden, every

Magic!

book that you've read, every video you've watched, every clinic you've attended, and every lesson you've taken will be illuminated in a blinding flash of comprehension. It is a miracle of meshing human and equine; you are truly the center of this powerful, magnificent creature—like magic!

This is dressage! This is dancing with your horse! And you will always and forever be seeking that blinding epiphany of dressage—a miracle of man and horse. This is why we don't quit. No riding experience that has come before can match those moments when you are actually achieving real dressage.

Is the Passion Worth It?

"Ah, dressage...that enigmatic journey that both frustrates and entices. If we pursue it honestly, it strips us of all illusions and self-righteousness that we might be holding on to. Our horses become mirrors to our souls, by which we can see our failures and frailties. It is then our choice whether to recognize and affect change in our very character or to cause our horses to bear our character flaws (which they will readily do because their capacity for grace is so far beyond our own). It is my belief that wisdom is a result of just such enigmatic exercises."

EquusTP "Dressage (Your thoughts please)," 1/1/04, UDBB

You will experience many emotions on your journey, from the heights of exhilaration to the depths of frustration and despair. But you will never, ever be bored. There is something very important in that. It's a fact that the final episode of the television show *Survivor* will lose its ability to enthrall you to same degree. You no longer live vicariously watching these ordinary folks attempting to achieve extraordinary things because you are personally engaged on your own journey of epic proportions. You no longer live on the side-lines—you are a participant in life. A rare achievement indeed.

Yes, dressage will engage you on many levels. This isn't just about riding a perfect 20-meter circle. This is not just about achieving harmony with your horse. This is about discovering new depths within yourself, aboard a creature as remarkable and generous as the horse. This is about having a passion!

Is it worth it? What have you really learned? What is the point? Or, as Ultimate Dressage member "sunrider" asks in a moment of despair, "Why have a passion that is so strong if you are so obviously never going to be good at it?"

Perhaps this is best answered by the closing words of another Ultimate Dressage member, "evasandor" who says, "About the passion, though ... if you could give up riding just because you weren't good at it, it wouldn't be a passion. It would be a diversion. Good passions are hard to come by!"

So true!

In Their Own Words

"I'm looking for support. This is probably the hardest time I've faced since I started dressage 13-odd years ago. I am not one for lack of determination. I have persevered for years with no money, cheap horses, trying to do it "right" and not resort to the quick-method trainers or gadgets or pushing the horse too quickly. I've been lucky enough to have one good trainer (for four years on and off) in that period. While I'm doing this, I watch my friends in draw reins and double bridles (beginners on Training Level horses), and they are progressing. I am having one of those periods where you think such things as, "What is the point? Why have a passion that is so strong if you are so obviously never going to be good at it?**"**

sunrider, "How to understand my horse's intelligence/personality (long)," 12/9/03, UDBB

"Nothing I've done in my life has made me feel as good or as bad as dressage! That includes a lot of years in graduate school and a demanding profession that I love. The understanding of self that's come to me from riding has been very powerful, both on good days AND on bad days.**"**
Vee, "Dressage (Your thoughts please)," 1/1/04, *UDBB*

"Horses understand how to be horses; it takes a long time for humans to become more 'horselike.' The human partner who, by the way, is supposed to lead the horse, is the one who takes the longest to learn. Horses know how to be horses; humans must learn the language of the horse and how it moves and responds to its environment. It takes many long, patient years for the human to learn how to ride/train/work with their horses.**"**
horseperson, "Why is it called 'horse training'?" 5/28/03, *UDBB*

"A rider has to bear in mind that he is not the teacher of the horse, but that through his understanding and feeling he trains and makes it possible for the horse to perform ... with ease, grace, impulsion and cadence—and in beauty and harmony.**"**
Fritz Stecken, *Training the Horse and Rider*

"The more I ride, the less I know. No kidding. It's like peeling an onion. You think you've arrived at the "centre," only to find yet ANOTHER layer. Not that I'm crying about it. But knowing there's more to learn, I think, is what's keeping me working towards an elusive perfection. Every time I find one of the many 'keys,' I find a new door.**"**
Apples, "Rider Learning Curve—never ending," 11/30/03, *UDBB*

"The aim of this noble and useful art is solely to make horses supple, relaxed, compliant and obedient and to lower the quarters without all of which a horse— whether he be meant for military service, hunting or dressage—will be neither comfortable in his movements nor pleasurable to ride.**"**
François Robichon de la Guérinière, *L'Ecole de Cavalerie*

"What I hope in the future is that everyone who gets on a horse does it with the humbleness, willingness to learn, and willingness to understand the horse and what he needs without the ego and the plans getting in the way. As I have learned more, my awe for my horses has increased. They are more generous to us than we deserve. If we recognize that and honor that, then the work will be good, the horses will not suffer needlessly, and competition becomes a celebration of that relation-ship.**"**
Dressagerose, "the future of dressage…," 8/2/02, *UDBB*

"I once was cussing out a horse for his stupidity, when one of my friends who was not familiar with horses asked me, 'If this horse is so stupid, why do you spend so much of your time, money and efforts on him? It seems to me that you must be the dumb one.' By the way, this is not an Arab proverb—it is a 20th century truth!**"**
John Winnett, *Dressage as Art in Competition*

"If we manage, throughout our training, to preserve both the gentleness and the gaiety of our horse, we shall not, in the end, go very far amiss. Horses really are sensitive to atmosphere. If we enjoy working with them and do so in a cheery frame of mind, in the spirit of learning and doing something together, they will respond generously."

Henry Wynmalen, *Dressage: A Study of the Finer Points of Riding*

"My emotions, and usually ugly ones, got in the way at one time in my life. I finally sat myself down and said, 'Why am I reacting like this with a horse I profess to love?' The answer lay within me. I was frustrated that I could not do with my horse what I felt I should be able to accomplish. It was not the horse. It was me because I really didn't know what I was doing. Never mind all the money I had paid for lessons. As I studied and found answers, I achieved the inner peace for which I was seeking."

Katherine, "Emotions in the way—please help!" 12/9/03, *UDBB*

"Just as not everyone can be a top athlete nor can every horse reach the top of its discipline. As the majority of riders are satisfied at being able to put up a good show in novice classes this has advantages. We should realize that this achievement can bring happiness and satisfaction and too many riders set their sights too high for themselves and their horses and thereby lose the happiness riding can bring them."

Reiner Klimke, *Basic Training of the Young Horse*

"One of my teachers once said, 'You ride how you are,' meaning that the manner in which people conduct themselves aboard their horses reveals their true personalities. I've found this to be true in my experience."

Lynne S, "Personalities and dressage," 12/14/03, *UDBB*

"Dressage is, perhaps, the most fascinating of horse sports. Its very name may seem strange to some people but really it means simply 'to dress' or 'to train.' What this actually entails is the training of a noble, responsive, trusting animal to carry himself in the best possible way.**"**
Jennie Loriston-Clarke, *The Complete Guide to Dressage*

"I ride because I like—even need—the place it takes me. For whatever reason, being around/on horses is a mental rush for me. I walk into the barn, and I can physically feel stress flowing away from me. I get on my horse's back, and the world melts away. The only clarity is the connection between me and my horse. It is purely selfish; and yet it is not. The people who must put up with me in their lives say I'm much easier to get along with when I'm riding. So it is a gift to them that I ride.**"**
Little Jamie, "A question of Intent—Warning: May Challenge or Inflame," 10/10/03, *UDBB*

"But for the most part, dressage is like making good bread, rather than eating a fabulous cake. You have to like the process.**"**
TSandM, "Is dressage fun," 10/17/03, *UDBB*

"I think dressage is so complicated that I do not yet even know HOW complicated it is. I'll admit to there being a time when I thought a round neck was dressage. Some novices probably still think that. I was a happier rider then.**"**
ToN Farm, "Is dressage complicated?" 10/12/03, *UDBB*

"If the art were not so difficult, we would have plenty of good riders and excellently ridden horses, but, as it is, the art requires, in addition to everything else, character traits that are not combined in everyone: inexhaustible patience, firm perseverance under stress, courage paired with quiet alertness. If the seed is present, only a true, deep love for the horse can develop these character traits to the height that alone will lead to the goal."
Gustav Steinbrecht, *The Gymnasium of the Horse*

"Sometimes we dressage riders obsess about 'perfection' (or someone's definition of perfection) and struggle to be perfect rather than being 'purposeless.' This can also apply to our live. Basically how I interpret this as applying to riding is to quit worrying about what others think, what you or others think is 'right' and start listening to the horse. I found that, for me, this came slowly over time, and as I started to be able to listen to the horse, I became able to "listen" to people much better."
pluvinel, "Taking a long hard look; soul-searching," 3/21/03, UDBB

"Dressage, to me, is taking a dream, turning the dream into a thought, turning the thought into an idea, and turning the idea into a dance. It's all about watching, listening, trusting, feeling, loving, hating, laughing, crying and knowing that you'll always go back for more. When you feel that you and your horse have become one, at the moment there's nothing else in the world but the two of you, you know there's nothing like it. When partnership and trust are invisibly formed into beauty and harmony … well, I could go on. But I'm sure none of it makes sense anyway. I'm the idealistic, romantic, bookwormish sort whom nobody understands."

JumperCash "Dressage is...," 1/16/04, *UDBB*

"I do believe one can overcome a lack of talent with training. Otherwise I would give up and go for a trail ride. This is a very, very difficult sport, one in which we raise the bar nearly every time we ride. Since we raise the standard all the time, of course we can rarely meet it. All we can do is meet an acceptable standard for today. It requires a special sort of mental space and acceptance."

Bliss, "riding, how much talent vs training?" 9/25/03, *UDBB*

"We all work SO hard at this. I think dressage riders have to be some of the most determined, focused and willing people in the world, but when we don't have the tools we are just wasting all that amazing determination, focus and willingness in futile attempts to reach a path that we don't have the tools to traverse."

EquusTP, "Santa Claus and the Substance of Dressage," 9/10/03, *UDBB*

"Dressage is the fundamental obedience training ... for the rider!"

Erik Herbermann, *Dressage Formula*

"The overwhelming question/feeling/mystique of dressage for me is that just when you think you have understood something you discover a whole new depth to that one feeling that you never knew was there. Just when you think you have it you realize you're only scratching the surface."

sunrider, "lighten up (warning—philosophical and long)," 9/7/03, UDBB

"Anyway, if the dressage world is getting you down, why not go trail riding for a few weeks? Or try jumping him? Or learn some of the ground games and play with your horse? Why not try clicker training him to do goofy tricks? Lie on his back facing his tail while he eats and read a book. Or, you could always just get rid of him; he is probably what is dragging you down ... LOL!"

class, "When the going gets tough...what do you do?" 8/5/03, UDBB

"Okay, we talk all the time about bad riding, and we've talked about good riding. But what makes a rider worthy of respect? The vast majority of us will not be a reprise of Reiner Klimke, but we are not despicable because of that ... To me, if someone approaches this demanding discipline with humility, seeks instruction, does research, and listens to the horse, that person is worthy of respect even if her skills never reach an advanced level."

TSandM, "Worthy of respect," 7/27/03, UDBB

Struggling with the Meaning of Dressage and Friendships

So there you have it, in the words of great masters, the great authors and in the language of everyday modern dressage riders. Dressage is both utterly fascinating and utterly frustrating. It consumes mere mortals and the most gifted of masters alike! How can you or I be any different?

Putting the journey into perspective goes a long way in dealing with those mostly frustrating and occasionally triumphant moments. You and I are not alone in our bewilderment. I've ridden horses on and off for most of my life—and now consider myself to be a beginner rider, again. Could this be what the masters are referring to when they speak of giving up your ego?

Given my limitations of time and money, my family responsibilities and my advancing age, I hold out little hope that I'll ever progress much beyond where I am today. So why bother? Because, first of all, once you've started down this path, it's impossible to erase what you've learned. Grrr. But more so, I know I've become a much better horseperson for the efforts I've poured into dressage.

After TFO's fabulous Intro Level season, I took him, for yuks, to a hunter/jumper schooling show. I

showed him in the pleasure division flat classes. I had
shown in a hunter show on maybe one occasion in my
far off youth, so this was pretty new to me. What a
revelation! It was so easy! After what seemed to be the
50th lap around the ring at a trot I thought, enough
already! Where are the transitions? Where are the
school movements? How do people do these endless
laps around the arena without a single 20-meter circle?

  TFO won the pleasure division championship at
that show. Surely you can now understand why I refer
to him as The Fabulous One! I do sometimes wonder if
the judges simply were overwhelmed by his mane and
tail. But, really, even our paltry attempts at Intro Level
dressage have paid off. I could never have duplicated
this effort in my Hack Stable Queen youth. It was only
through the Olympic-sized angst poured into my Intro
Level horse that I could achieve, for me, the once
unachievable. My understanding of riding and horsemanship is so much greater.

  But still, winning an Intro Test or a pleasure
class doesn't make progressing in dressage any easier.
It's still and always will be a struggle. I've achieved
some wisdom in learning to back off when it starts to
get too overwhelming. TFO is my third dressage horse,
and he is the horse of dreams. He is so beautiful he
takes my breath away. How can I do him justice? The

worst for me is knowing, absolutely, TFO would be so much farther along with a better rider. Perhaps it's the old fallen away Irish Catholic guilt thing and has nothing to do with dressage! Could be—but I doubt it!

But does TFO really care? I know he cares when I'm frustrated and short-tempered. Oh yes, he's exquisitely attuned to my emotions! I know he cares about getting breakfast and dinner on time. I know he cares about his best buddy in the whole world, our Nokota, Chico. But does he care about being a Grand Prix horse? Does he care about showing and winning? Or, in the words of Paul Belasik in Riding Towards the Light have I merely "made a deal with the devil" that has nothing whatsoever to do with dressage and my wonderful TFO? Do these profound questions keep me up at night? You betcha—sometimes!

I cherish those friends I've made on the battlefield of dressage—my comrades in arms—my fellow adult amateurs. One of my favorites is Holly. I knew she was too awesome because she owns and rides a leopard Appaloosa in dressage. A really, really loud Appaloosa! She's definitely making a statement there! Holly is a wonderful, versatile rider with a gift for having fun. She has successfully done dressage, horse trials, hunters and foxhunting with that very same extravagantly marked mare. Pretty cool indeed!

Holly has shown me the path to enjoying pace events and even trying my hand at combined tests. That's right—she showed me that when the going gets too tough with dressage, go have fun! The only thing I don't like about Holly is that TFO is guaranteed to be ignored when in the company of her extremely loud Appaloosa! Invisible, I'm telling you, even with his mane and tail! Obviously, I still need to work on the "ego" thing.

There have been other, surprising friendships. Like Judy, who is ultra-dedicated to the art of dressage. She owns and rides a Lipizzaner, so you know she's serious. We met through clinics with the trainer from the Other School. Yet, despite her seriousness about dressage, she is remarkably supportive and revealed a wonderful fun side.

Judy, my daughter and I once went on a truly memorable trail ride. We were hacking along on our rare, never before combined threesome—an Andalusian, a Nokota and a Lipizzaner—through the hills and dales of southeastern Pennsylvania, when we came upon members of the local, landed gentry likewise enjoying the day with their four-in-hand coach. What an extraordinary event in our otherwise ordinary lives! They had stopped for refreshments and urged us to join them. We had a fabulous time! Really, we couldn't decide who was more noteworthy—us or them! We even determined that our horses were "champagne broke." Yes, a four-in-hand coach comes equipped with an almost full service bar, including champagne! This is the stuff memories are made of!

And finally, there is my dear friend Pam; my fellow Hack Stable Queen alumna. You might wonder what happened when we went on our fabulous adventure—to look at the horse of her dreams-her dressage prospect. If nothing else, I hope I've established that Pam's angst about buying her dream horse and the entire dressage journey is not an isolated, slightly schizophrenic event! Quite the opposite. Pam's anxiety makes absolute sense to struggling dressage riders everywhere!

Yes, Pam bought that horse we traveled six hours to see. Pam, who was fascinated by Andalusians long before their recent surge in popularity, now owns the horse of her dreams. And so, some 30 years later, she is finally the proud owner of a beautiful bay Andalusian gelding named Brio. Like everything to do with dressage, it's a matter of being careful what you wish for! Now she must struggle, like we all do, to take satisfaction in the everyday reality of owning a dream, and surviving this art form called dressage. Yes indeed, we are all quiet heroes in this quest for the perfect 20-meter circle. ■

"About the passion, though: If you could give up riding just because you weren't good at it, it wouldn't be a passion. It would be a diversion. Good passions are hard to come by! Wear it proud! I have a laugh at myself now and then ... like, here I am riding like ka-ka but hey, at least my horse is really clean. ...

(cue pompous orchestral soundtrack)

*SO! Crappy but determined riders everywhere, unite. A few geniuses may shine at the top of the iceberg, but WE are the whole rest of that massive, majestic structure. In every barn, all over the world, we toil away with our grumpy bend-free horses and creative seat positions!! If it were not for our brave example as we ride—year in and year out!—the selfsame 20-meter circle, no one would know what natural talent is. LOL!!!!***"**

evasandor, "How to understand my horses intelligence/person-ality (long)," 12/9/03, *UDBB*

Books and Web sites of Reference

The Books

Basic Training of the Young Horse by Reiner Klimke

Centered Riding by Sally Swift

Cross-Train Your Horse by Jane Savoie

Dressage as Art in Competition by John Winnett

Dressage Formula by Erik Herbermann

Dressage in Harmony by Walter Zettl

Dressage: A Study of the Finer Points of Riding by Henry Wynmalen

Enter at A, Laughing by Brian McKeown

The Gymnasium of the Horse by Gustav Steinbrecht

More Cross-Training by Jane Savoie

My Horses, My Teachers by Alois Podhajsky

Riding Towards the Light by Paul Belasik

The Complete Guide to Dressage by Jennie Loriston-Clarke

Training the Horse & Rider: A Book of Dressage by Fritz Stecken

The Web sites

www.nokotahorse.org–The Nokota Horse Conservancy, Inc.

www.teamnokota.com–The Official Members Organization of the Nokota Horse Conservancy, Inc.

www.ultimatedressage.com–The Ultimate Dressage Bulletin Board (UDBB)

www.4germanshepherds.com/Dysplasia.htm–Hip Dysplasia in German Shepherds

www.aboveandbeyond-eac.com–Helene Asmis Clifford at Above and Beyond Equestrian Arts Center *www.agdirect.com*–Horses for Sale

www.amazon.com –Dressage Books

www.angelfire.com/sports/dressage/pages/Karl.html–Karl Mikolka's "Karl's Corner"

www.bn.com–Barnes and Noble, Dressage Books

www.ccec.net–Paula Kierkegaard (also known by her UDBB screen name "galopp")

www.chioaachen.de–Facts and Figures: Equestrian Sports in Germany

www.classicaldressage.com–"Famous Quotes" and "Classical Riders"

www.classical-dressage.net –Classical Dressage with Sylvia Loch

www.dieoff.org–Fossilgate-the impending end of the Petroleum Age.

www.dreamhorse.com–Horses for Sale

www.dressagedaily.com–Dressage Competitions and other neat stuff

www.dressageworld.com–"Famous Quotes" and "Classical Riders"

www.ebay.com–Search for old copies of the TV series Kung Fu

www.geocities.com/dressagereaders–The International Dressage Reading Institute

www.kahlin.net/noir/dressyr/rollkur/rollkur.php–"Deep" explained

www.michaelmoore.com–Author's favorite author

www.moveon.org–Politically incorrect views from the ultra-liberal tree-huggers

www.paulbelasik.com–Paul Belasik and Moonlight Park

www.realgsd.info/–GSDinfo/Papers/SV/breedsurvey.htm#warden German Shepherds in Germany

www.spanische-reitschule.com–The Official Web site of the Spanish Riding School of Vienna

www.horsesport.org–FEI Official Site, (Fédération Equestre Internationale)

www.usdf.org–U.S. Dressage Federation

www.usef.org–U.S. Equestrian Federation - Rules - XIX: Dressage

www.wbstallions.com/wb/swana/articles/EMILY.HTM–Diagonal Advanced Placement

DISCLAIMER

I have included many quotes throughout *Survival Guide* from a variety of sources. One of the most fascinating resources I have tapped into is the Ultimate Dressage Bulletin Board (UDBB), an online dressage Web site. The folks at UDBB have been, almost unanimously, very supportive of my project. I extend my heartfelt thanks for all their support and encouragement. However, I must hasten to add that the views expressed in this book are mine and mine alone. This book is not affiliated with UDBB, except for the generosity of the various members who agreed to let me use, or abuse, their words.

The same goes for other sources I've quoted—including dressage masters and highly respected authors of dressage books. I've liberally used and abused them as well, for the sake of finding humor in the serious world of dressage. I've made mention of, and sometimes named, people I've encountered personally during my journey. While I may poke some fun, I wish to be clear that I hold the utmost respect for these people and for their dedication and knowledge of dressage. Any failures to achieve the shoulder-in and the left lead canter rest solely upon my shoulders—regardless of how much I'd love to pass the blame! And finally, I hope the citizens of Germany and the members of the Spanish Riding School of Vienna will forgive me. As I'm sure you're aware, it's just sour grapes!

Please keep in mind that this book was written with tongue firmly in cheek and hopefully, all in good fun. Any mistakes I have made or liberties I have taken in this book are completely my own.—M.A.O. ❏

UNITED STATES *Dressage* FEDERATION, INC.

USDF
Introductory
Level Test

2003
INTRODUCTORY LEVEL — TEST A

(UNITED STATES PONY CLUB D-1 TEST)
Walk—Trot

A

USPC D-1 Test

This unique series of tests provides an opportunity for the horse and/or rider new to dressage to demonstrate elementary skills. The tests have been designed to encourage correct performance and to prepare the horse for the transition to the USA Equestrian tests.

Instruction:

All trot work to be ridden rising. Transitions from walk to trot and trot to walk may be performed through sitting trot with the objective of performing a smooth transition. Turns from center line to long side and long side to center line should be ridden as a half circle, touching the track at a point midway between the center line and the corner, and vice versa.

Comment:

Horses should be ridden on a light but steady contact, with the exception of the free walk in which the horse is allowed complete freedom to lower and stretch out the head and neck.

AVERAGE TIME

6:00 Standard Arena
5:00 Small Arena
(Possibly longer for schooling shows)

DVCTA Dr. Sch. Show - 8/17/03
Radnor - Judge: Ann Forer
45 - USDFA - Capricho
Margaret Odgers

_____
Number and Name of Horse

_____
Name of Rider

MAXIMUM POSSIBLE POINTS: 200

FINAL SCORE

153   76.500

Points   Percent

UNITED STATES *Dressage* FEDERATION, INC.
220 LEXINGTON GREEN CIRCLE • SUITE 510 • LEXINGTON, KY 40503
PHONE: 859/971-2277 • FAX: 859/971-7722
E-MAIL: USDRESSAGE@USDF.ORG • INTERNET: WWW.USDF.ORG

_____
Name of Judge

_____
Signature of Judge

229

USDF INTRODUCTORY LEVEL — TEST A
(UNITED STATES PONY CLUB D-1 TEST)
2003
(Walk—Trot)

REQUIREMENTS:
Free walk
Medium walk
Working trot rising
20 meter circle at B & E
Halt through walk

NO. 45

		TEST	DIRECTIVE IDEAS	POINTS	COEFFICIENT	TOTAL	REMARKS
1.	A	Enter working trot rising.	Straightness on center line.	7		7	Straight
	X	Halt through medium walk. Salute - Proceed medium walk.	Quality of gaits and smoothness of transitions.				
2.	C	Track right medium walk.	Balance and smoothness of turn, and quality of walk.	7		7	nicely forward
3.	M	Working trot rising.	Balance and smoothness of transition. Quality of trot.	7		7	obedient
4.	B	Circle right 20 meters, working trot rising.	Quality of trot, roundness of circle.	8	2	16	Steady rhythm nice bend
	B	Straight ahead.					
5.	Bet- ween B & F	Medium walk.	Balance of transition, quality of walk.	8		8	ditto
6. K-X-M		Free walk.	Quality of walks. Straightness and freedom of free walk. Transition.	9	2	18	
	M	Medium walk.					
7.	C	Working trot rising.	Balance and smoothness of transition. Quality of trot.	6		6	give forehand in transition to avoid stiffening
8.	E	Circle left 20 meters, working trot rising.	Quality of trot, roundness of circle.	8	2	16	try to maintain steadier connection
	E	Straight ahead.					
9.	A	Down Centerline.	Straightness on centerline, quality of trot, halt and transition.	7		7	drifting slightly R into straight halt
	X	Halt through medium walk. Salute.					

Leave arena in free walk. Exit A

COLLECTIVE MARKS:

Gaits (freedom and regularity)	7	1	7	
Impulsion (desire to move forward, relaxation of the back)	7	2	14	
Submission (attention and confidence; harmony, lightness and ease of movements; acceptance of the aids with nose slightly in front of the vertical.)	8	2	16	
Rider's position and seat; correctness and effect of the aids.	8	3	24	

200

FURTHER REMARKS:

LOVELY HORSE!
TIME TO MOVE UP!!

230